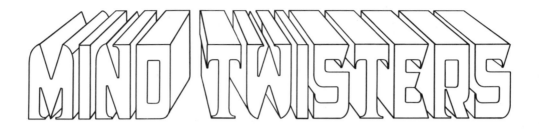

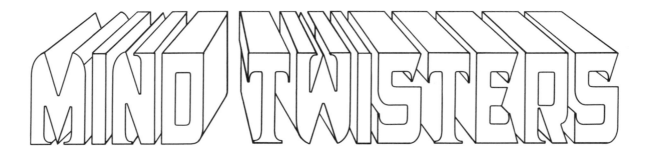

MIND TWISTERS

◆ Godfrey Hall ◆

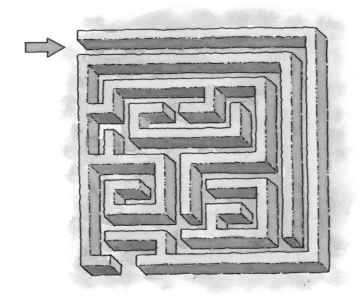

Random House 🏠 New York

First American edition, 1992

Copyright © 1991 by Grisewood & Dempsey Ltd.
All rights reserved under International and Pan-American
Copyright Conventions. Published in the United States by
Random House, Inc., New York. Originally published in Great
Britain by Kingfisher Books, a Grisewood & Dempsey Company,
in 1991.

Library of Congress Cataloging in Publication Data
Hall, Godfrey.
Mind Twisters / by Godfrey Hall.
p.   cm.
Includes index.
Summary: Presents puzzles, experiments, optical illusions, card
tricks, things to make, secret codes, number tricks, and more.
ISBN 0-679-82038-8 (trade); ISBN 0-679-92038-2 (lib. bdg.)
1. Scientific recreations—Juvenile literature. 2. Science—
Juvenile literature. 3. Science—Experiments—Juvenile literature.
[1. Scientific recreations. 2. Science—Experiments.
3. Experiments.] I. Title. II. Title: Mind Twisters.
Q164.H24 1992
793.8—dc20
91-27688

Manufactured in Hong Kong   10   9   8   7   6   5   4   3   2   1

INTRODUCTION

In *Mind Twisters* Godfrey Hall has gathered together an exciting collection of tricks, puzzles, scientific experiments, magic tricks and things to make. You will learn unbelievable facts. You will also find out about great scientists, what they did and how they made their discoveries. You will be challenged by the experiments and puzzles. And the card tricks and other feats of conjuring will dazzle your friends and amaze your family.

Mind Twisters is divided into six sections. Each one is filled with a different type of brain-contorting challenge. In the section on psychology you can learn how memory works and try to improve your own. The section on technology looks at structures — how they are built and how they stay up. You can build different types of bridges and see which can carry the heaviest load. The section about science tells you about time, space, communications and the slowest mammal on earth! The final chapter reveals how to get an egg into a bottle without cracking the shell and tells all about the magic hexagon.

Mind Twisters is a book to dip into, to browse through and to enjoy for its hours of entertainment. It contains hundreds of fascinating facts to uncover. Some are extraordinary, some funny, some thought-provoking. Some are simply baffling. But they all are lively, stimulating and varied, and they will keep you entertained wherever and whenever you open this book.

CONTENTS

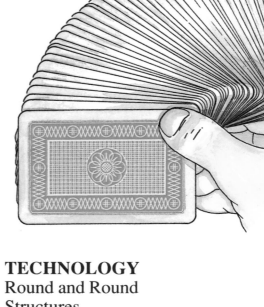

SCIENCE

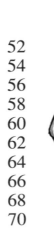

NATURE

PUZZLES

ODD MAN OUT

Take a look at the people around you, at a bus stop, or perhaps people waiting to get into a movie. Everywhere you look, you will notice that people are all different (unless there are any identical twins about!). See if you can spot the "odd man out" in these puzzles. Some are easy, but others may be more challenging!

ANSWER THIS

A woman went into a shop and bought a coat and a hat. The coat cost $100 more than the hat. The two together cost $150. How much did the hat cost?

Percy said, "I am the same relation to your son as Jack is to you." "That's right," said Fred. "And you are the same relation to me as Jack is to you."

What is the relationship between Fred and Jack?

THE NUMBERS GAME

There are lots of amazing things that you can do with multiplication. Write down the seven-times table from one to ten. You only need to write the answers, as shown below.

7	42
14	49
21	56
28	63
35	70

Now add the digits together in each number. If you get two digits as an answer, then split them and add them again.

7	6
5	13... $1 + 3 = 4$
3	11... $1 + 1 = 2$
10... $1 + 0 = 1$	9
8	7

Look carefully and see if you can spot any pattern emerging from these numbers. Now try again with another table, such as the eight- or six-times. Can you find a pattern?

Now try with the nine-times table. You will find the answers quite interesting!

FUN WITH NUMBERS

"How many marbles do you have?" asked Poppy. "Well," said her brother Malcolm, "if Robert gives me four, then he will only have half as many as Deborah. But if Deborah gives me four instead, then the three of us will have the same number of marbles." How many marbles did they each have to start with?

The total weight of a container of flour is 40 ounces. After the baker uses one-third of the flour to make some bread, the container and flour weigh 28 ounces. How much does the container that holds the flour weigh?

How many minutes is it past eight o'clock if 74 minutes ago it was half as many minutes past seven?

ODD MAN OUT

Here are some number sequences that have the last two numbers missing. See if you can work out what the missing numbers are.

Easy ones:
2; 4; 6; 8; 10; 12; ___; ___
5; 10; 15; 20; ___; ___

A little harder:
2; 4; 7; 9; 12; ___; ___
2; 9; 13; 20; 24; ___; ___
12; 15; 9; 12; 6; ___; ___
20; 15; 22; 17; 24; ___; ___

Very difficult:
9; 27; 6.75; 33.75; 5.625; ___; ___
1,000,000; 500,000; 166,666.66; 41,666.66; 8333.33; 1388.88; ___; ___

Find the "odd man out" in these numbers:
69; 333; 159; 735; 452; 17,367.

CAN YOU WIN?

Here is a problem you can challenge a friend with. In front of you place a bowl containing six marbles. The object of the game is to be the last person to take a marble from the bowl. Each player takes turns alternately and can take either one or two marbles per turn. If you offer to let your friend go first, will he or she win?

The winner of the game is going to be the person who is left with one or two marbles. It follows that the winner will be the player who leaves his or her opponent three marbles. Whether the reply to this is to take one or two marbles, will you always be left with an amount you can clear in one turn?

If your opponent takes the first move, and takes one marble, take two yourself. There will then be three marbles left and you can win on your next turn. If your opponent takes two marbles, then take one yourself. This again leaves three marbles and you will win on your next turn. Your victims will soon find out that the kind offer to start the game was not so well meant as they thought and that they will always lose.

THE DAISY GAME

A man named Sam Lloyd thought up this puzzle a long time ago. He enjoyed making up chess problems as well.

You will need two people for this. Find a daisy and take turns pulling off either one petal or two petals side by side. The first person takes one or two petals, the second person now takes one or two petals directly opposite those taken by the other player. The game goes on until there are no more petals left. The winner is the one who takes the last petal.

QUITE A PUZZLER

This is a puzzle that you can try on your friends.
Ask someone to think of a number.
Tell him or her to add seven.
Multiply by two.
Subtract four.
Get your friend to tell you the answer.
If you divide the number by two and subtract five you will get the right answer every time.

CALCULATOR FUN

What can you use your calculator for? When you go shopping you could take a calculator with you so that you know exactly how much the bill will come to before you get to the cashier. Calculators can be fun as well as useful. Here are some ideas for games you can play with your calculator. Happy calculating!

BEGINNINGS

It was the Chinese, or maybe the Babylonians, who invented the abacus. This was one of the earliest and simplest forms of adding machine, and it is still used today in parts of China, the U.S.S.R. and Japan. The word comes from the Latin *abacus*, meaning ''a board covered with sand for tracing calculations.''

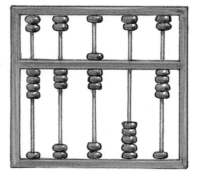

An abacus is made up of a wooden frame with movable beads that are on rods. In 1834, an Englishman named Charles Babbage designed a calculating machine that was so complicated that it could not be built! He did manage to make a model of it, however. The machine had lots of wheels and columns and was worked by turning a handle.

In 1945, two Americans named J. Presper Eckert, Jr. and John Mauchly came up with the ENIAC. This stands for **E**lectronic **N**umerical **I**ntegrator **a**nd **C**omputer. It was like a giant calculator.

WORDS AND MORE WORDS

Calculators can add, subtract, divide and multiply, but if you are clever, you can also make them talk! Let me explain.

Put the number 3 into your machine. Turn the calculator upside down and you will find that it has turned into an E. Now try these numbers and see what they give you when you turn the calculator upside down:
0.7734

Now put these numbers into the calculator and see what you come up with:
3507 ... Did you win or lose!
505 ... Help!
5663 ... Cluck, cluck!
5338 ... Buzz, buzz!
577345 ... On the sand or in the sea?
You could send some coded messages to your friends and tell them to decode them using their calculators.

HOW DOES IT WORK?

Calculators are small but complicated pieces of equipment. They are usually powered either by a battery or by solar cells, which are fueled by light energy. Underneath the keys of your calculator are printed circuits. When you press a key down, it closes contacts in these circuits, which sends messages to the microchip. The microchip acts as a "brain," interpreting information from the keys and sending instructions to the display.

The display on a calculator is made up of straight lines. When all the lines on the display are showing, they make up a row of number eights. The display is probably either LCD (Liquid-Crystal Display) or LED (Light-Emitting Diode). LCD does not light up but looks like numbers written on a piece of paper. Depending upon the electrical signal received, the LCD either blocks out or allows light through, forming the numbers that you see on your display. The diodes in an LED calculator glow when electricity is fed to them.

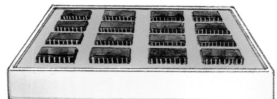

PURE GENIUS

Calculators are powerful machines.

Here are some puzzles for you to try out on your calculator.
1. Multiply $10 \times 9 \times 8 \times 7 \times 6 \times 5 \times 4 \times 3 \times 2 \times 1$.
2. Divide 10,000,000 by 5. Now multiply the answer by 10.
3. What are some ways of making 224, using only four numbers? (For example, 16×14.)

Here is a game you can play on your own with a pack of cards.

Shuffle the pack and deal yourself three cards. Each card from 2 to 10 is worth its face number. The jack is worth 11, the queen 12, the king 13 and the ace 14.

See how far you can get in three steps.

Put the value of the first card into your calculator — for example, 4. Now choose × or ÷ or + or −. Put in the value of the second card — for example, king (13). Now choose ×, ÷, +, or − again and put in the value of the last card. Press the equals button. What is your answer?

Now see if you can find the highest and the lowest number using the same three cards.

THINK OF A NUMBER

Think of four numbers — for example: 8, 3, 4, 2. Now combine them to make the largest and the smallest number: 8432; 2348.

Take the smaller from the larger:
$8432 - 2348 = 6084 \ldots$

Make the largest and the smallest combinations of this new number: 8640; 0468. Subtract the smaller from the larger. Answer: 8172.
Now do it again . . .
$8721 - 1278 = 7443 \ldots 7443 - 3447 = 3996$.
Keep going. Will you ever end up at 0?
Now try these numbers:
8, 3, 2, 6. What happens?

SOMETHING LIKE SNOOKER

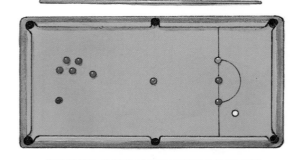

Yellow: 2 points. Number for score: 56
Green: 3 points. Number for score: 144
Brown: 4 points. Number for score: 156
Blue: 5 points. Number for score: 192
Pink: 6 points. Number for score: 268
Black: 7 points. Number for score: 299

You will need two players and a calculator. The first player enters a two-digit number. The second player tries to get the same number by entering a multiplication sum. For example: 48; $12 \times 4 = 48$ is correct. 97; $12 \times 8 = 96$: off by one. To pocket a red, the answer must be correct or only off by one.

If the second player pockets a red, he or she can go on for a colored ball. This is done by putting in the two numbers for the totals shown in the table. These must be exact to score. There are six reds in this game. Each is worth one point when it is pocketed. The six colors are worth the number of points shown in the table. If a color is pocketed, then the player goes for another red and repeats the process. When all the reds have gone, then the colors are pocketed in point order.

The winner is the player with the most points at the end of the game.

PAPER PUZZLES

Here are some puzzles that are easy to do but difficult to explain. Some of them are what is known as optical illusions. This means that something is drawn or appears in such a way as to make your eyes play a trick on you. The thing you are looking at is actually not what it seems. The lines below are a good example of an optical illusion.

THE MÖBIUS STRIP

Möbius was a German mathematician who was born in the 18th century. This is his strip, which is quite amazing! You will need a piece of paper about 14 inches long and 2 inches wide, some glue and a pair of scissors.*

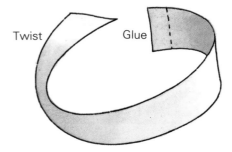

Twist the paper once and glue the ends together.

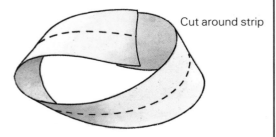

Cut around the center of the paper as shown. Let the paper go and see what happens. It doesn't seem possible, but it is. Cut the paper again.

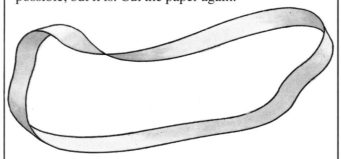

Try the same experiment with a thicker piece of paper and see how long you can make your strip.

LINES THAT CONFUSE

Take a piece of paper and draw two parallel lines exactly the same length, about 2 inches long and ¼ inch apart.

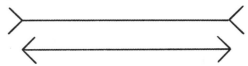

Now draw two lines at either end as shown. Show them to someone and ask them which line is longer. They are, of course, both the same length, but they don't look it!

Here are some more confusing lines. Draw three parallel lines, 2 inches long and ¼ inch apart.

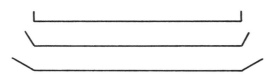

At the end of each straight line draw angled lines as shown. Show them to a friend and ask him or her which is the longest straight line.

NETWORKING

Try to draw these without taking your pencil off the paper or going over any line twice.

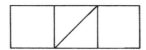

You will find that if there are more than two or three intersections, the network cannot be completed without taking the pencil off the paper. Which of the patterns below cannot be drawn as a network?

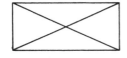

*Ask an adult to help you.

PUZZLE

This puzzle was invented by Edouard Lucas, a French mathematician. It was produced as a toy in 1883. It is called the Hanoi Tower and it is possible — you just have to think about it!

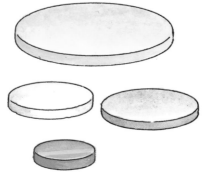

Find four lids of different sizes. Put two of the lids on the table as shown at X. Now see if you can rebuild the pile without putting the larger lid on top of the smaller one. You must move the lids, one at a time, via the midpoint, Y.

How many moves did it take?

Now try the same thing, this time with a pile of three lids. You must only move one lid at a time and you must not put a larger lid on top of a smaller one.

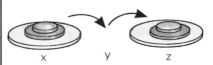

With two lids it takes a minimum of three moves, with three lids it takes seven moves. Try it with four lids. How many moves did it take this time?

AMAZE-ING

See if you can find your way out of these mazes. Hampton Court, in southern England, has a famous maze. At one time mazes were popular with British garden designers; you can often find them at English country houses with large gardens.

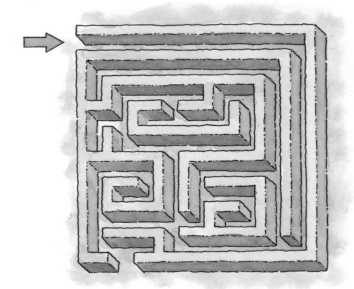

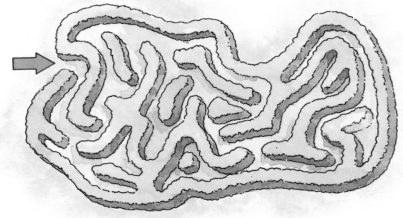

TANGRAMS

Puzzles with shapes – triangles, squares, parallelograms – are always fascinating and can be very tricky. They are good for baffling your friends and for making interesting patterns.

TANGRAMS, TRIANGLES, AND TESSELLATIONS

A tangram is an ancient Chinese puzzle, invented thousands of years ago, in which a square is cut into a parallelogram, a square and five triangles.

This is how you do it. Take a piece of cardboard and draw a 4-inch square. Using the pattern shown here, cut the square into seven pieces.* You will have two large triangles the same size, one medium-sized triangle, two small triangles, a square and a parallelogram.

See if you can make:
1. A large triangle using any three pieces.
2. A large rectangle using all of the pieces.
3. A square using two triangles.

When you have finished, give the pieces to someone else and ask him or her to put them back into a square without looking at the picture above.

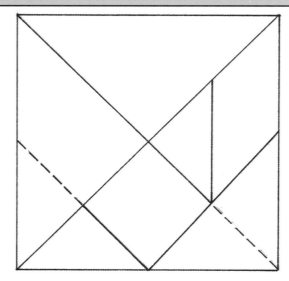

TANTALIZING SQUARES

Take a 4-inch square of paper and fold it down the middle. Fold it again and keep on folding until it is impossible to go any further. Open up the piece of paper and look at the shapes you have created. Can you see the squares within squares? Color in some of the squares so that they stand out.

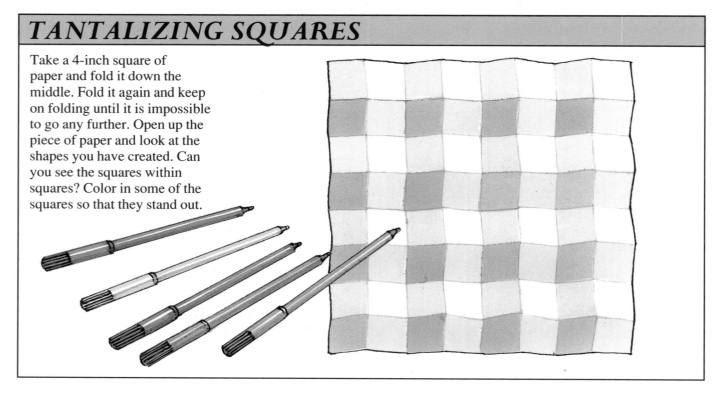

*Ask an adult to help you.

PATTERNS AND PICTURES

Take your 4-inch square of paper and fold it as before. When you have finished, cut out some of the patterns you see in it.* Use the triangles to form your own patterns. Here are some examples:

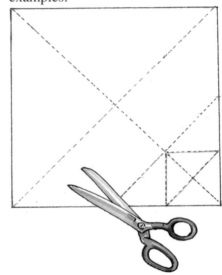
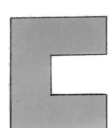

TESSELLATIONS

A shape that tessellates is one that can be repeated without leaving spaces in between. An equilateral triangle will tessellate and so will a square, but a circle won't.

Make your own pattern using shapes that tessellate. Here are some examples:

TRICKY TRIANGLES

Here are some numbers in triangles. See if you can work out which triangle contains the largest and which contains the smallest number when you add all the digits together.

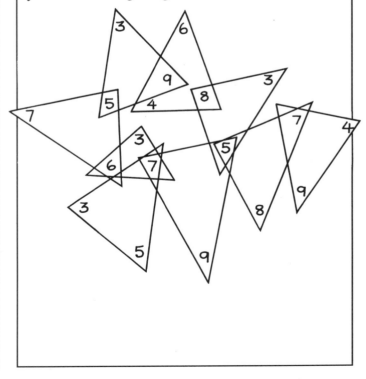

MAGIC NUMBERS

Playing around with numbers and number patterns can be fascinating. Throughout history people have experimented with numbers and their patterns. Why not try out some of these on your teachers at school? Or how about using carefully measured squares to copy a picture at twice the original size? These pages show you how!

THREE IN A ROW

John Napier was a Scotsman who was born in the 16th century. In 1614 he published a table of numbers called logarithms. These helped people multiply and divide by simple addition and subtraction!

The original numbers were cut into pieces of bone and formed a set of rods. These were used for multiplication and division. They became known as "Napier's bones." This process helped Napier to invent logarithms.

Make up two "bones."

Make sure you add the bones on the slant.

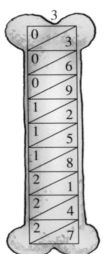

For quick multiplication or division, place them side by side and read them off:

Make another bone, this time the three-times table:

Now put the three bones together, as shown.

You can now multiply by 53.

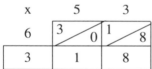

so 6×53=318

MAGIC SQUARES

This is a magic square. If you add up the numbers down, across or diagonally you will always get the same answer.

See if you can work out the numbers that are missing from these magic squares.

Baffle your friends by making up some of your own.

4	9	2
3	5	7
8	1	6

12	7	14
		9
8		10

15	8	1	24	17
16		7		23
	20		6	4
3	21	19	12	
9	2	25	18	11

IT'S A MYSTERY

This is a number puzzle that you might like to try out on someone.

Draw a square and number it as shown.

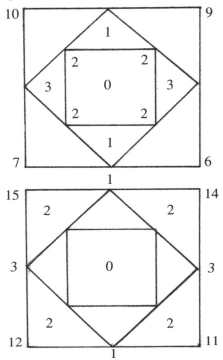

Now take the smaller number away from the larger on each side, put your answer in the middle and draw another square as shown. Do this again and you will find that you always end up with 0.

Ask your friends to think of another number — for example, 15. Number the square in the same way, and your final answer will be 0!

BIGGER IS BETTER

Find a picture that you would like to make larger. Copy it, using a piece of tracing paper. Divide your picture up into carefully measured squares; then draw another grid twice the size of the first. Copy each square of the first drawing onto the second grid. When you have finished you will have a picture twice the size.

TWO CAN PLAY

A game for two players.

Choose a number from the square. Enter a number into the calculator that you think will produce the number in the square after it has been multiplied by 16. If you are correct, cover the square over with a small piece of paper. The first person to make a straight line with pieces of paper is the winner.

80	112	32
128	160	64
96	144	48

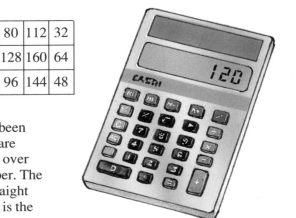

THREE ROWS

See if you can rearrange these numbers so that each side adds up to 15.

1	2	3
8		4
7	6	5

NUMBER FUN

Some of these ideas are good fun for those wet and miserable days when you have to stay indoors. Have you ever tried mind reading?

It is quite difficult, but here are one or two ways you can get around the problems.

SEVEN, FIVE, THREE

This game can be played with fifteen coins. Lay out the coins. The winner of the game is the one who forces the other person to pick up the last coin. Each player takes turns picking up coins. You can pick up as many as you like, but they must be from the same row. See how well you do.

MIND READING

Mind reading isn't so difficult if you try this idea at your next party. Go out of a room and get a friend to stay in the room. Get someone else in the room to select a card from six playing cards. Go back into the room and tell your friend to hold up each card. Have him or her say that you will be able to select the correct card. You will be able to do this really easily.

Make sure that your friend knows the system. Have him or her say "Is it this one?" before each card but the chosen one. When your friend gets to that card, have him or her say, "Is it that one?"

You could also have your friend scratch his or her ear before the right card or always choose the third card. See if you can work out your own silent code.

PUZZLES

Hold a pack of cards downward in the shape of a fan and get someone to select a card. As the person takes out the card, open the pack slightly and note which card — say, the ace of spades — is at the bottom of the top half. Get the person to put the card back in the opening. Then allow anyone to cut the pack. You will be able to find the selected card, as it will always be the card in front of the ace of spades. Another way of doing this is to shuffle the cards and then note the bottom card.

Hold the pack facedown in your left hand. With your fingertips slide the bottom card back a few inches and with your right hand throw down the second to bottom card on the table facedown. Continue to do this and say you want someone to shout stop. At that point the next card will be the one you use for the trick. When you hear the word *stop*, pull out the card you have been holding back and put it on the table, giving its name as you do so.

THE DICE GAME

Throw down four dice onto the table and cover them up with your hands. Put them side by side and remove your hands.
Now get a friend to say what the total is of the four sides that are touching. Write down the answer. If your friend is right, he or she gets a point. Next your friend throws and you guess.

Another way to play this is to guess what numbers are on the hidden sides of the dice based on the visible numbers on the opposite sides. For example, if four is showing, then what is on the other side?

You can do really well at this game if you can memorize the positions of the numbers.

NUMBERS GALORE

Now try these.

30 × 30	80 × 80
50 × 50	90 × 90
70 × 70	100 × 100

How did you do? Can you think of a quick way to do these? Here it is:

3 × 3 = 9 plus two 0's
5 × 5 = 25 plus two 0's
7 × 7 = 49 plus two 0's

There are a number of quick ways of checking out numbers. Here is another.

ODD + ODD = EVEN
7 + 3 = 10   233 + 343 = 576
EVEN + EVEN = EVEN
6 + 6 = 12   444 + 326 = 770
ODD + EVEN = ODD
3 + 4 = 7   341 + 566 = 907
EVEN − ODD = ODD
8 − 5 = 3   680 − 655 = 25

What do you get if you multiply an odd by an even, an even by an even and an odd by an odd?

HOW MUCH?

Collect some items such as a book, a pencil, an eraser, a cup, a pair of shoes, a tie, a scarf. Find out how much each of them would cost if new. Then get some friends to guess how much each one would be. See how far off they are. Now make up some tags with the correct prices of the items, mix them up and see if your friends can match the goods with the price. If you want to make it really difficult, put the value of the goods in a foreign currency and see if they can sort them out now.

Find a list of exchange rates for different currencies from a daily newspaper. Find out how much 50 cents would be worth in five different currencies on one particular day. How many German marks would you get, and how many French francs?

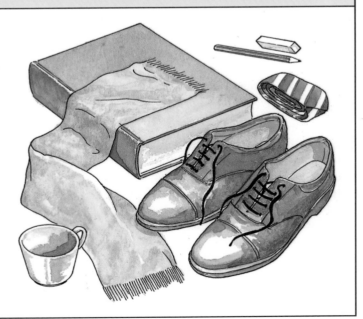

ROUND AND ROUND

If you spin around too fast and for too long you will probably feel very dizzy and fall over. That probably won't happen when you try out the ideas below. Try out the windmill on a still day and on a windy day to see what difference the wind makes. The spinning seed will behave differently depending on the height you throw it from and on how windy it is where you are. There are lots of other spinners you can make – so start thinking.

COLOR

The Englishman Sir Isaac Newton discovered that white light is made up of seven colors. He found that if you paint these seven colors onto a piece of cardboard and then spin it, the colors will all blend together to make white. You may want to try this yourself.

To make a color spinner, make a cardboard circle with a radius (distance from the center to the edge) of three inches. Cut it out and divide it into seven more or less equal sections.*

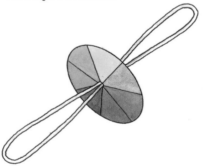

Color these red, orange, yellow, green, blue, indigo (blue-violet) and violet. Make two holes in the cardboard circle and thread a piece of cord through them. Tie the ends together and twist the cord around until it is tight. Pull your hands outward and watch what happens.

COLORED SPINNERS

You can make a selection of other spinners using different colors.

Cut out a cardboard circle and draw a line dividing it in two.* Color one side blue and the other green. Put a pencil through the middle of your spinner or use a cord as described in **Color**. Spin the circle and watch what happens. Now try these combinations and see what happens:

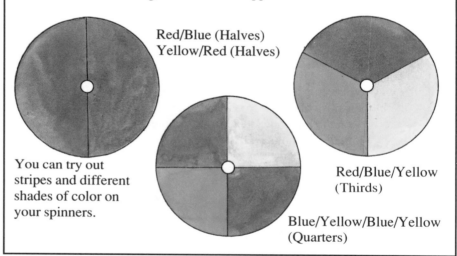

Red/Blue (Halves)
Yellow/Red (Halves)

Red/Blue/Yellow (Thirds)

Blue/Yellow/Blue/Yellow (Quarters)

You can try out stripes and different shades of color on your spinners.

MORE SPINNERS

It is possible to make your own paper helicopter using a piece of cardboard.

Cut out the cardboard as shown,* add a paper clip and let it fall. Add another paper clip to the bottom if you have any problems with it. The weight helps to balance the helicopter.

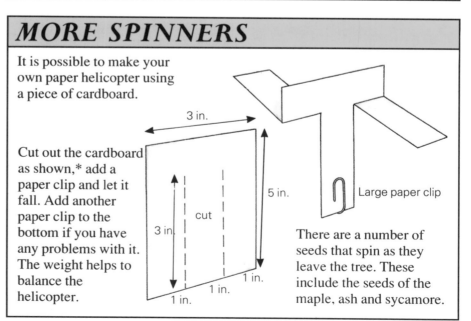

3 in.

5 in.

Large paper clip

3 in.

cut

1 in.

1 in.

1 in.

There are a number of seeds that spin as they leave the tree. These include the seeds of the maple, ash and sycamore.

*Ask an adult to help you.

GAMES

There are a number of games you can play using spinners. Cut out a piece of cardboard with six

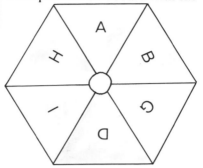

equal sides.* Divide it into six sections and put a letter in each. Push a pencil or a used matchstick through the middle.

Spin the wheel and watch where it lands. Ask someone to give you a two-letter word starting with that letter. Spin again, but this time the word must be three letters, and so on. You each take turns. The game ends when you get to the point where you are unable to think of a word with the correct number of letters.

SPINNER TESTING

Test out some of your spinners to see which are the most successful. Make up a selection of different-sized circles and also sticks. Mix them up and try them out. Do long sticks and small circles work better than short sticks and large circles?

Try out other shapes as spinners, such as squares and triangles. Do they work as well as circles?

When you have finished your tests, use your results to design a really good spinner and see how long you can make it spin.

WINDMILLS

Windmills are used today to power generators to make electricity. The blades that spin around in the wind are attached to a shaft, which turns the turbine.

This is a simple windmill that you can make yourself.

(i)

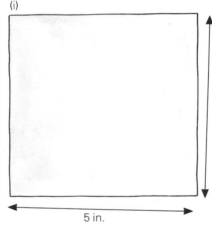

5 in.

5 in.

Cut a square of paper 5 inches by 5 inches.

Cut along the dotted lines as shown.*

(ii)

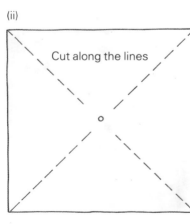

Cut along the lines

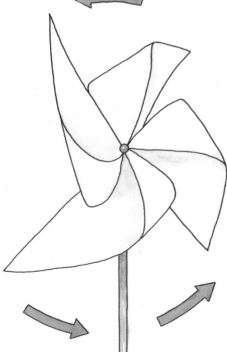

Fold over the corners from the edge to the middle and stick them down. Fix the windmill to a stick with a pin. Put a bead in between the stick and the windmill to help it spin.

STRUCTURES

If you climb to the top of a tower or stand on a bridge well up above the trees and buildings, you can usually get a good view of the ground below for miles around. Some towers have an observation deck on top from which you can get a great view. If you take binoculars with you, you will be able to see even farther than with the naked eye.

TOWERS

A tower is usually a tall square or circular structure that can form part of another building. Your local church, for example, may have a bell tower, or a castle may have watchtowers. It is important that towers be strong so that they don't fall down. Years ago people built them out of stone and brick, but nowadays a variety of materials are used, including concrete and steel.

You can build your own tower using either rolled-up newspaper or drinking straws (see the top of the next page).

When building a tower, remember that this shape . . .

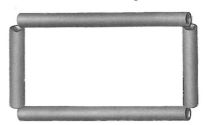

is not as strong as this shape.

The final design must be strong, but at the same time it must be as light and stable as possible.

TALL TOWERS

People are continually building taller and taller structures. For a time the Empire State Building in New York was the tallest building in the world, at 1,250 feet. The Sears Tower in Chicago has 110 stories and at 1,454 feet is the tallest building in the world. The radio mast at Plock, Poland, is even taller, rising 2,120 feet above the ground. One of the tallest structures in Britain is the Telecom Tower, which is just over 623 feet tall. The Radio and Television Tower in Berlin is over 427 feet high and is called "the Lump" by the locals. The CN Tower in Toronto, Canada, rises 1,822 feet.

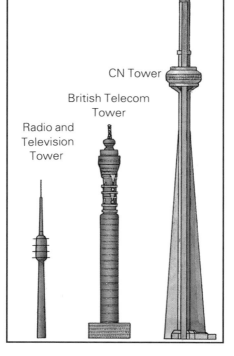

CN Tower

British Telecom Tower

Radio and Television Tower

OLD TOWERS

The Leaning Tower of Pisa in Italy was built in 1174. Unfortunately, it was built with a foundation that was too shallow for the soft ground and so the tower began to sink. The builders tried to correct the angle of the building, but they were unsuccessful. It is 180 feet tall, and is about 16 feet out of line.

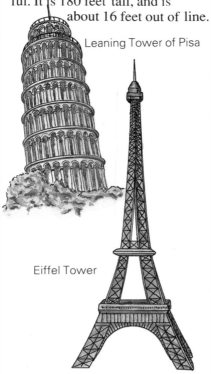

Leaning Tower of Pisa

Eiffel Tower

The Eiffel Tower in Paris is 984 feet high and was designed for the Paris Exposition of 1889. It is an impressive structure and a popular tourist attraction. In 1909 it was nearly pulled down, but it was saved at the last minute. The top of the tower serves as a base for a light beacon and weather station.

TOWER POWER

Take a box of straws and see how high you can build a tower. Remember to use triangular frameworks, as these will make your tower much stronger. Make sure that the base is firm and that the points where the straws join are secure. One way to do this is to fix the straws together by sliding pipe cleaners inside.

When you have finished, test out your structure by blowing on it. Does it remain upright or fall over? Another good test is to see how much weight it will hold. Put your weights on carefully and a few at a time; otherwise the tower will keel over and collapse.

If you can't get any straws, then make your tower out of rolled-up newspaper. Again, use triangular shapes as you build it higher.

BRIDGES

Another structure you can try to build is a bridge. The Golden Gate Bridge in San Francisco is a "suspension bridge." You can make a suspension bridge by cutting two balsa-wood towers and joining them with two pieces of string across the top.* Then make string loops all of the same length and tie them onto the two strings. When you have enough loops, slide in a long piece of thick cardboard or balsa wood to complete your bridge.

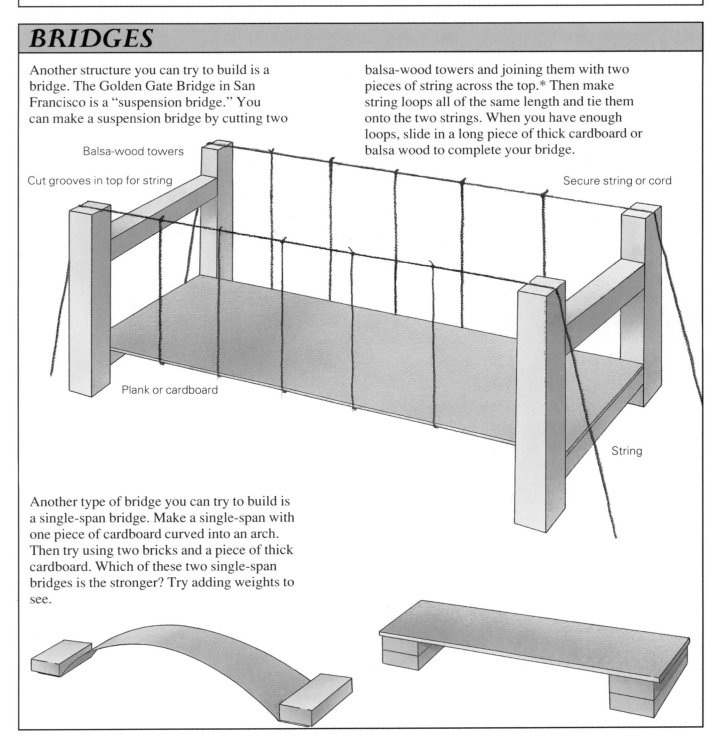

Balsa-wood towers

Cut grooves in top for string

Secure string or cord

Plank or cardboard

String

Another type of bridge you can try to build is a single-span bridge. Make a single-span with one piece of cardboard curved into an arch. Then try using two bricks and a piece of thick cardboard. Which of these two single-span bridges is the stronger? Try adding weights to see.

*Ask an adult to help you.

POP-UPS

The ideas on these pages will save you money as you make your own pop-up cards, masks and glasses, which you can give as presents.

Try out some of your own paper-engineering ideas once you have had some practice at these.

POP-UP CARDS

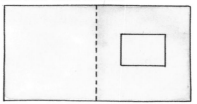

1. Take a piece of thin cardboard 12 inches by 8 inches and fold it in half lengthwise.
2. Fold over the top, as shown.
3. Open it up and paint on an image — say, a head. Allow it to dry.
4. Cut out around the head.*
5. Fold it back down. When you open the card the head will pop up!

CUT-OUTS

Take a piece of thin cardboard 8 inches by 12 inches and fold it in half lengthwise.

Draw one of the shapes shown below on your card. Make sure that you draw away from the crease.

Cut around the shape and color in your card.* It will stand up if you bend it in the middle.

WINDOWS

Window cards are great fun. Take two pieces of thin cardboard that are the same size and fold them in half.

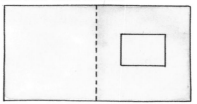

Draw a square or rectangle in the middle of one of the pieces.

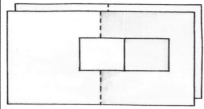

Cut out only three sides of the shape.* Glue the top piece of cardboard onto the bottom piece and fold the flap back.

Decorate the window or draw a picture inside.

*Ask an adult to help you.

HEADS UP

Take a piece of cardboard 8 inches by 12 inches and roll it into a tube.

Glue down the edges. Decorate the front of the tube with a face and add on ears and a nose.

Now cut out a hat from thin cardboard, including a tab on the top.*

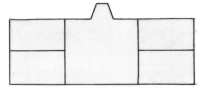

Fold the hat as shown and push it into the tube face.

When you pull the tab, the hat pops up. You could try making a magic snake or a clown instead of a face and hat.

MASKS

Masks are easy to make, and a simple design can be used to create a spectacular effect.

Cut out a strip of cardboard 2 feet long and 2 inches wide. Put it around your head and cut it to the right size. Leave an overlap to glue the strip together.

Now cut a shorter piece of cardboard 16 inches by 2 inches and fit it over your head.*

Cut out a piece of cardboard 8 inches by 3 inches and make two eyeholes in it together with a V-shape for your nose.*

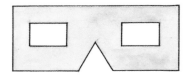

Now decorate your mask with cardboard, feathers, paints, seeds or sticky paper.

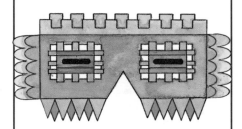

Fit the mask onto your circle of cardboard and try it on.

POP-OUTS

Pop-outs are cards that pop out at you when you open them up. Take two pieces of thin cardboard or paper 8 inches by 12 inches and fold them in half. Take one and draw a line from the middle of the creased edge toward the middle of the cardboard for about 2 inches.

Cut along this line, making sure that you start from the creased edge.*

Hold the cardboard in your hand and fold back both edges to make two triangles. Push the triangles through to the inside of the cardboard. The two triangles now form a mouth. Draw in your creature or face around the mouth. Glue the other piece of cardboard onto the back and decorate it.

*Ask an adult to help you.

FLYING SURPRISES

The first passenger-carrying hot-air balloon was launched in France by the Montgolfier brothers in 1783. It was made out of linen and traveled a few miles. Here are some flying surprises you can make yourself.

MAKING A PARACHUTE

To make a parachute:

1. Take a piece of thin paper 6 inches square.
2. Cut four pieces of thread, each 6 inches long.
3. Attach the strands of thread to

the corners of your piece of paper, using cellophane tape or glue.

4. Join the strands of thread using a small piece of modeling clay.
5. Throw your parachute up into the air and watch how it falls.

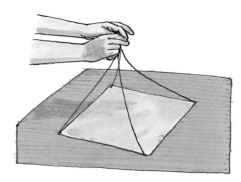

Try out some different types of material for the parachute canopy, such as an old handkerchief, and try weights other than modeling clay.

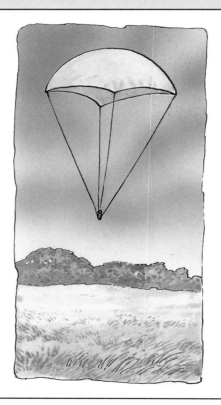

HELICOPTERS

The first modern helicopters were designed in the 1930s. Today, they are used for a variety of jobs, from lifting sick and injured animals from mountaintops to air-sea rescue and rounding up cattle.

To make a helicopter, take a swizzle stick and push it through a square piece of cardboard. Twist the card, give it a spin and watch it fall.

Throw it into the wind and watch what happens.

SEEDS

The seeds of the maple tree work like helicopter blades. They spin as they fall to the ground and can be carried a long way by the wind.

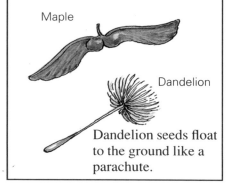

Maple

Dandelion

Dandelion seeds float to the ground like a parachute.

MAKING PAPER PLANES

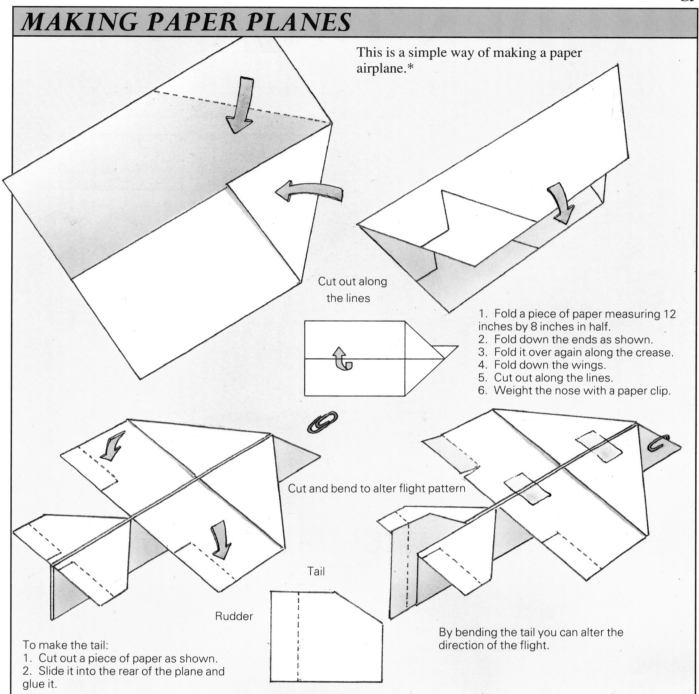

This is a simple way of making a paper airplane.*

Cut out along the lines

1. Fold a piece of paper measuring 12 inches by 8 inches in half.
2. Fold down the ends as shown.
3. Fold it over again along the crease.
4. Fold down the wings.
5. Cut out along the lines.
6. Weight the nose with a paper clip.

Cut and bend to alter flight pattern

Tail

Rudder

By bending the tail you can alter the direction of the flight.

To make the tail:
1. Cut out a piece of paper as shown.
2. Slide it into the rear of the plane and glue it.

CONCORDE

The Concorde first flew on March 2, 1969. It travels at twice the speed of sound and can fly from New York to London in under three hours instead of the usual flying time of a passenger aircraft of around six hours. The Concorde is designed so that it will cut through the air without much wind resistance and has specially shaped wings that help it fly at high speeds. When it is about to land or take off, the nose drops so that the plane can get enough lift.

The Concorde II will be lighter, use less fuel, have a longer range and carry more people.

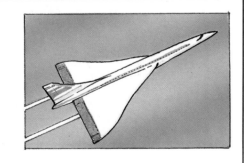

*Ask an adult to help you.

HIDDEN TREASURE

ALL IDENTICAL

Which of the planes below can be made from the objects below?

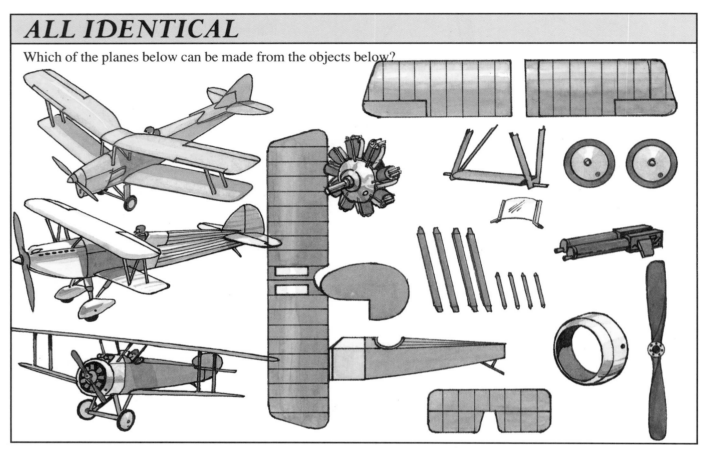

TEACHER'S PROBLEM

Can you help the principal of Boot Lane School? All the classes must be in separate rooms, and she can only have four straight partition walls built. The middle classroom must be square.

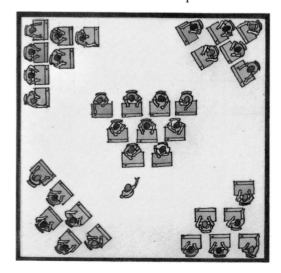

ALL THE SAME?

Which of the galleons below are identical sister ships?

1.

2.

3.

4.

5.

6.

CAPTAIN BLACKHEART'S TREASURE

Jake and Kate were exploring the attic of their great-grandfather's house. The house was once owned by Captain Blackheart, the infamous pirate whose vast treasure had never been found. Jake was staring down as the sea crashed against the wild and rugged coast below, when Kate shouted out.

She had found an old sea chest. Among the ragged old clothes was a cutlass, a strange-looking compass and a tattered piece of paper. Kate held up the paper, but it fell to pieces. She stared hard at the faded writing and gasped as she recognized the signature at the bottom.

While Kate tried to fit the pieces together, Jake was fencing with the cutlass. Suddenly he yelled as the handle fell off the cutlass. Inside was a yellowed piece of paper. Jake gingerly unwrapped it. It was a map. Jake and Kate looked at each other in amazement. Were they about to discover where Captain Blackheart's treasure was hidden?

Can you help them?

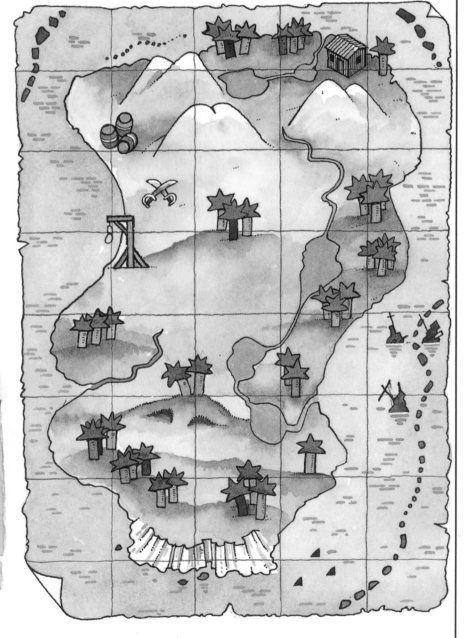

We had sailed for many leagues over uncharted seas until the lookout cried "Land Ahoy". Up ahead was the uninhabited and unmarked island where I buried my treasure.

I moored our good ship, the Black Boar, in the place you'd not like to stay. I gave the rest of the crew double helpings of grog, and went ashore with two trusty swabs and the treasure. We headed in the direction the skeleton points until reaching a lake. Then we turned towards the way the spyglass sees and reached the base of one of the three twin peaks.

From here we marched the way the parrot flies until reaching the sea. We followed the coast line and buried my treasure in the third palm grove we came to.

Blackheart

MODEL POWER

The ancient Chinese were some of the first people to use rockets. A rocket works by burning fuel, which produces gases. The gases are forced backward out of the rocket, thrusting it forward. The fuel that was used to power the Apollo moon mission weighed as much as 70 large heavy trucks!

You only have to use simple bits and pieces to make the models shown here.

WHOOSH!

You can make a jet engine.* You will need a balloon, two chairs, some cord or string, two toilet-paper roll holders, a diswashing-liquid top or a bulldog clip, a couple of pieces of cardboard and some cellophane tape.

Cut a length of cord about 6 feet long. Blow up the balloon and fit the dishwashing-liquid top onto the end. Make sure that no air is escaping from the balloon. Stick on the cardboard and toilet-paper roll holders as shown. Tie the cord between two chairs and pull it tight. When you are ready, open the clip and let the air rush out. Watch what happens to your jet engine as it moves along the cord. See if you can improve this design in any way.

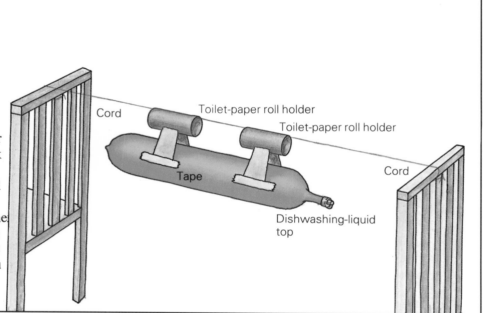

Cord

Toilet-paper roll holder

Toilet-paper roll holder

Tape

Cord

Dishwashing-liquid top

GLIDE

If you are interested in sailing boats, you might like to try this.* The power for your boat will come from the wind.

Find a polystyrene tile and cut it out into the shape of a boat. Make a tiny hole in the center, making sure that it does not go right through. Otherwise your boat might sink!

Find a short piece of doweling rod or balsa wood and fit it into the hole. Attach a sail made from a piece of thin paper. Launch your boat into the sink or bathtub and see how fast you can make it go by blowing on the sail.

If you can find a tiny piece of camphor, attach it with a piece of cord to the back of the boat. When the boat touches the water, it will move of its own accord.

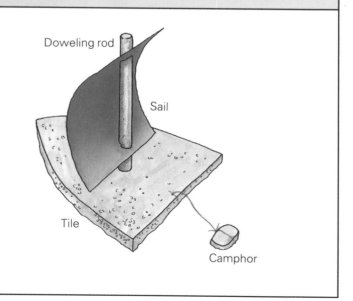

Doweling rod

Sail

Tile

Camphor

*Ask an adult to help you.

SPLASH!

This is a simple type of paddle wheel. Cut out the shape of a boat from a piece of balsa wood.* Attach a rubber band to a tiny piece of wood. Fit the paddle so that it is in the middle of the gap and fix the rubber band to the back of the boat with two thumbtacks. Twist the rubber band until it is tight. Hold the paddle and put your boat into the water. Let it go and watch what happens. If the boat goes backward, try twisting the rubber band the other way.

TRUNDLE ...

There are many different ways of making simple vehicles. Here are two that you can try.

Find a small cardboard box and glue on some thick cardboard brackets at each corner. Make a hole in each bracket and through the box to hold the axle.* Collect four spools and two pieces of doweling rod. Push one of the spools onto the end of the doweling and put a tiny piece of modeling clay on the end to keep the spool from falling off. Slide the rod through the two holes as shown and fix on another spool. Do the same at the back. Now test out your vehicle. See how well it goes down a slope.

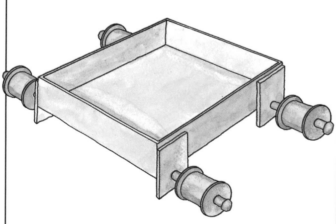

For this buggy you will need a ruler, two bulldog clips, four spools and some doweling rod. Set it up as shown below and slide in the wheels.

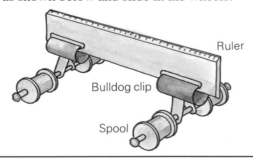

Ruler

Bulldog clip

Spool

A SPOOL TANK

You will need a spool, a rubber band, two matchsticks and a slice of candle with a hole in the middle. Ask an adult to cut this for you.

Attach half a matchstick to one end of the rubber band and push it through the spool. Push the rubber band through the hole in the piece of candle and slip it around the other matchstick. Make sure that this end is secure. One way to do this is to cut a groove into the candle before you start so that the matchstick can sit in the groove.

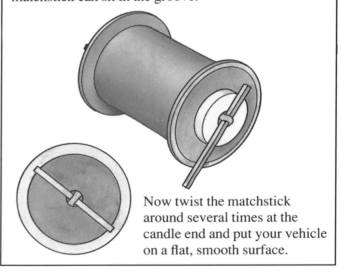

Now twist the matchstick around several times at the candle end and put your vehicle on a flat, smooth surface.

WHICH IS BEST?

Now try out some of your vehicles using a ramp made from a piece of wood and several books. See how well they move. Which one moves the smoothest and which one the quickest? Do they move better on carpet or on a smooth surface? See if you can design your own vehicle along the same lines as the spool vehicle using a dishwashing-liquid bottle, an elastic band and a piece of wire.

*Ask an adult to help you.

THINK BACK

How's your memory? Can you remember what you had for dinner yesterday and last week? Some of these ideas will test how good your memory really is. There are also some handy ideas for helping you to remember things by making a list. And you can also read about some unsolved mysteries from the past, like the case of Dr. Mitchell and the dutiful daughter, or the deserted ship the *Mary Celeste*.

WHAT IS MEMORY?

Your body contains millions of neurons. These are tiny nerve cells that transmit and receive electrical impulses. The control center for all this activity is the central nervous system, which is your brain and your spinal cord. The bones of your spine protect your spinal cord from being damaged.

The left side of your brain deals mainly with language, facts and figures, whereas the right side is concerned with music, art and color. The brain also organizes and stores things that you have seen, heard, felt and tested. This is your memory.

LOOK BACK

Stop for a moment and see how much you can remember about yesterday. What did you do from the time you got up until the time you went to bed? What food did you eat? Write down what you can remember.

Now think back a week. Can you remember what you were doing then? Where were you and who were you with?

Take one more step backward to a year ago. This will probably be more difficult. What were you doing a year ago today? Were you doing something special?

BACK IN THE PAST

Some strange things have happened in the past.

Take the case of the *Mary Celeste*. This was a completely deserted two-masted ship found out at sea in 1872. There was a good supply of water and food, and in the captain's cabin the table was laid for breakfast. It was as though the ship had suddenly been abandoned. The official explanation was that the crew had killed the captain and his family. But there was no sign of a struggle. Others have said that the crew was sucked up by a terrible wind, while others think that something rose from the sea and took the crew.

The disappearance of the crew is still a mystery and has yet to be solved.

Here is another mysterious tale.

It was a cold winter's evening in the last century when an American doctor, Dr. Mitchell, settled himself down by the fire after a busy day. Suddenly the doorbell rang, and standing by the door was a thin, ragged girl. She told him of her sick mother, who needed help. The doctor went to the woman right away and made her as comfortable as possible. He told her that she had a very kind daughter. The woman turned to the doctor and said, "But my daughter has been dead for a month, doctor. Her shawl and shoes are in that closet." The doctor looked and found them dry and warm. He turned to find the girl, but there was no one there.

THE TRAY TEST

This is a good way of seeing how effective your short-term memory is.

Put ten items on a tray and cover them with a cloth. Put the tray in front of a friend and take the cloth off for 30 seconds. Tell your friend to try to remember as many things on the tray as he or she can.

After 30 seconds ask him or her to tell you what was on the tray. Change the items and increase the number to twenty. See how many your friend can remember this time. You take a turn and see if you can remember all twenty.

LISTS

Making lists is often a good idea. It is helpful if, at the beginning of the day, you make a list of things to do, arranged in order of importance. As you go through the day, cross things off your list. If you are lucky, you will cross everything off your list.

You can often remember things from a list. Try this:
Make a list of things. Think of the first letter of each of the words and make a picture in your mind of something unusual beginning with that letter. For example, let's say you have to remember chicken on your shopping list. Think of a "peg word" for chicken such as "catch." The image you now have in your mind is of two chickens playing catch. Try this out with a list of twenty-five items and see how many you remember.

List of things to DO.

1. Pay 50¢ I owe to John

2. Stick wheel back on my model car

3. Collect Roger Rabbit from

4.

NAME GAME

Make up a set of labels with the names of famous characters on them. Fix each one on the back of a friend. Make sure that they don't see what's written on their label. Now the puzzle is for everyone to work out who they are. They can ask questions but others in the group can answer only yes or no.

TRY TO REMEMBER

Have you ever tried to remember last thing in the evening something you were told first thing in the morning? This can be very difficult. Do you have a good memory for names and faces? Do you know how your memory works? Some of the ideas below are designed to improve your memory and explain how it works. If you are worried that you might forget something important, try these tricks and techniques that will help ensure that you don't forget. You can also read about an amazing feat of memory.

HOW DOES MEMORY WORK?

You store information in your brain. As the information enters the brain it is remembered in four different ways. The sensory memory holds information for just a few seconds. The short-term memory will store about seven items at once, but will forget them in 30 seconds. Some things are moved from the short-term to the medium-term memory. You might want to remember someone's name for a short time. It will go into

this compartment. The fourth area is the long-term memory. This holds information for years and years.

NAMES, FACES AND NUMBERS

How good is your memory for faces and names? Look at these faces and the names underneath.

Turn to the back of the book and look at the five faces. Can you put a name to each one?

John Burns   Betty Broadwater   Tony Long   Rita Richards   Mervin White

Peter Johnson   Sheila Wright   Gordon Rivers   David Brown   Ruth Wong

See if you can remember these six phone numbers. Look at them for a few minutes and then close the book.

764-8796	678-9090	343-2323
432-1835	656-0056	427-0001

Which were the easiest to remember and why?

LINKING

You can train yourself to remember names, lists and information. One way is by "linking." This involves creating pictures in your mind.

If you want to remember a shopping list, you try to form a strong image in your mind of each item on the list. The first thing on the list may be a bag of flour. Imagine this in your mind floating in the air. Now link this to the next item, a string of sausages. The bag of flour breaks open and covers the sausages. When all the items are linked together, see if you can remember them all. If you have forgotten any items, rethink that part of the link.

KEEP FIT

You can help improve the power of your mind by always taking an interest in things and by making sure that you are paying attention. You must concentrate on whatever you are doing, and if you don't understand something, you should go over it until it is clear. You need to exercise your mind if you want it to improve.

JOGGING YOUR MEMORY

There are lots of different tricks and techniques to help you improve your memory. If you think you are going to forget something, make sure you write yourself a note, or tie a string around your wrist. You need to give yourself a visual reminder. If you remember something just before you go to sleep, move something in the bedroom – a chair or an ornament, for example. In the morning it will act as a visual reminder.

One good trick is to change around something that you always wear. Move a ring from one finger to another or wear your watch on the other wrist. When you look at your hand or wrist, it will jog your memory.

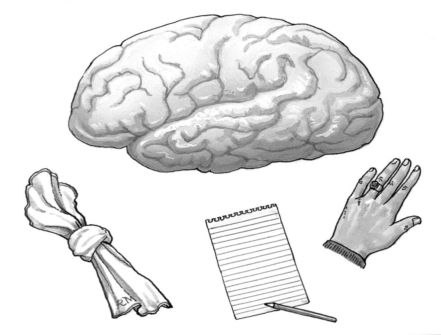

MNEMONICS

Mnemonics are verbal devices that help you to remember things. They are named after the Greek goddess of memory, Mnemosyne. There are lots of rhyming mnemonics — for example, "*i* before *e* except after *c*, or when it sounds like *a*, as in neighbor and weigh." There are also mnemonics that use the first letters of each word as a reminder: "Roy G. Biv" gives you the colors of the rainbow, in order: red, orange, yellow, green, blue, indigo, violet.

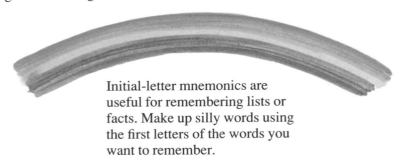

Initial-letter mnemonics are useful for remembering lists or facts. Make up silly words using the first letters of the words you want to remember.

PLATO

Plato, the Greek philosopher, compared the mind to a block of wax. As people experience things, these experiences make a mark on the wax and become memories. Eventually the

memories are worn away and disappear.
You also have to be careful that you don't forget old material as you learn new information. This can sometimes happen if the two things are closely linked.

Legend has it that elephants never forget. No one knows exactly where this idea comes from. One possible reason could be that in India it is said that an elephant will always recognize its owner.

A LONG POEM

When E. Titchener was only eight years old, he was able to remember a poem 244 lines long. He could still remember the poem 52 years later.

TRUE OR FALSE?

Sometimes it is very difficult to prove whether something is true or false. If it is true, we say it is fact. If it is false, we say it is fiction. UFOs and other strange happenings may all be true or may all be false.

This page is full of amazing facts and stories. Some of them are fact and others are fiction. Can you work out which are which?

RACE COURSE MADNESS

Horatio Bottomley had a brilliant idea for making lots of money. He decided that he would back every horse in a race, make sure that every one finished in the correct order and be sure that he owned all the horses in the race.

He hired six English jockeys to ride for him, and he decided to put them in a race in Belgium. The race was to take place at a seaside town on the coast that is famous for its sand dunes. He gave his orders to the jockeys before the race. Unfortunately, during the race a thick sea mist came in off the coast and everything went wrong. The jockeys all got muddled up and they ended the race in the wrong order.

Horatio lost an amazing amount of money and was ruined.
True or false?

BOOK FACTS

Here are some facts about books. See if you can figure out which are true and which are false.

1. A book was returned to an American library in 1968 that had been taken out in 1823. True or false?
2. The heaviest book in the world weighs 2,188 pounds. True or false?
3. C. S. Lewis wrote *Charlie and the Chocolate Factory*. True or false?
4. One of the best-selling books in the world is the Bible. True or false?
5. One of the slowest-selling books in the world sold, on average, only one copy in 139 days. It was published in 1716 and only 500 copies were printed. True or false?

FACT OR FICTION?

Here are some interesting facts about the world in general. Which ones are true and which are false?

1. The Andes are in Central Asia.
2. The Pacific Ocean is the largest ocean in the world.
3. The capital of Poland is Warsaw.
4. The tallest mountain in the world is in the Alps.
5. New York is farther north than Helsinki.
6. The island of Krakatoa in Indonesia blew up in 1883.
7. There are wind farms in California.

8. Penguins can be found living in the wild in Indonesia.
9. It would be possible to save over 30 million trees every year if most of our waste paper was recycled and used again.
10. Mount Everest is three miles high.

A GRAVE FACE

This all took place about twenty years ago. There was once a village in Spain where strange things started to happen. In one of the houses in the village a face appeared on the tiles of the floor. It was the face of someone in pain. The family tried to clean it off the floor without success. The floor was ripped up and replaced by concrete, but the face appeared once again. Workmen dug up part of the floor and found an ancient cemetery below. More faces appeared and special microphones recorded mysterious voices and noises in the room. No one has ever managed to explain why it happened. True or false?

DIFFICULT TO EXPLAIN

Unidentified Flying Objects, or UFOs, have been seen all over the world throughout the centuries. Many of the sightings have been explained. Some are still mysteries, however. For example, there was the case of the disk-shaped objects seen by Kenneth Arnold in 1947. He was flying a plane over Washington, D.C., when he saw nine strange flying disks.

Some people believe that UFOs are spaceships containing visitors from outer space. But some people have tricked others. In one famous case, hubcaps from a car were thrown into the air and photographs taken. This tricked a number of people who believed that some new UFOs had been spotted.

A TOUR

In England, mystery tours are popular. You go on a prearranged tour but you have no idea where it will take you. A couple went to Wales for vacation and decided to take a mystery tour. The tour took them back to their home town, Margate, in England. How about that for a mystery tour.

IS IT POSSIBLE?

Puzzles and tricks can be really mindbending. For example, some tongue twisters seem impossible to say. Even pictures can seem so confusing and puzzling that they are nearly impossible to work out. Look at the drawings to the right by the Dutch artist M. C. Escher. At first they look confusing, but can you work out why they are so strange?

NATURAL STRENGTH

At first some problems seem impossible to solve, but once you start to think about them clearly, you suddenly find that they can be done.

Some things in nature seem impossible too, such as the stories of gorillas so strong that they could bend rifle barrels and push down trees.

There is even one case of an explorer who watched a group of gorillas tossing boulders about as they were looking for food. When the gorillas had left, the explorer tried to lift one of the boulders. He could lift it only a few inches off the ground.

Another story about the strength of a gorilla comes from the Ringling Brothers Circus, where a gorilla was tested against fifteen men in a tug-of-war. According to this tale, the gorilla pulled the fifteen men right up to his cage with one hand!
How many of these impossible things can you do?

TONGUE TWISTERS

Tongue twisters have been around for many years. Do you know "Peter Piper picked a peck of pickled peppers"? This was first printed in 1819 in a book called *Peter Piper's Practical Principles of Plain and Perfect Pronunciation*. See if you can say all of these tongue twisters quickly ten times:

Freddy thrush flies through a thick fog.
Sally sells seashells by the seashore.
Stop chop shops selling chopped shop chops.
Still the sinking steamer sank.
Saucy Sally says Simon seems somewhat stupid sometimes.

Which one of these is the most difficult to say?

CAN IT BE DONE?

Shaun had a bag of 122 pieces of candy to give out at his party. His sister Sarah handed them out. When the bag came back, it was completely empty. Sarah, who was good at math, noticed that a third of the children had taken two pieces each, three of the children had taken three and the rest of the children at the party had each taken one.

How many children were at Shaun's party?

POOR PERSPECTIVE

No single part of this picture is illogical, yet the picture as a whole does not make sense. Start at the waterwheel and follow the water along its conduits and to the top of the waterfall. It tumbles down to turn the wheel – and starts its course again. A drop of water leaving the bottom of the fall would miraculously flow to the top. Also, the two towers seem to be equal in height, yet one has three stories while the other has only two.

In this picture Escher's hooded figures are continuously walking along a staircase that has no end. The problem is that although they appear to be climbing they always seem to be at the bottom. If they walk in the opposite direction they are walking down but always ending up at the top!

A LITTLE MATH

It is possible to multiply by the number 9 using just your hands. Number your fingers one to ten from the left. Decide how many times you want to multiply nine, then bend down that finger. Now count how many fingers are left on either side and this will give you the answer.

For example, $9 \times 4 = ?$ Bend down the fourth finger on your left hand. Count the number of fingers to the left (3) and those to the right (6). Answer $9 \times 4 = 36$.

ROOTS

Can you complete these words without using a dictionary?

GERAN---   TU---

DANDEL---   DA---

SUNFLO---

CHRYSANTHE---

PA---   R---

PETU---   MARIGO--

MUSICAL RUBBISH

Making music is great fun and you don't need much equipment to do it. In fact, most of the things you need can be found around the house. You can make whistles from straws or even a guitar from a tissue box and some rubber bands. Here's how!

MAKE A WHISTLE

The wind section of an orchestra is made up of instruments that we blow, such as flutes and oboes. Here is an easy way to make your own wind instrument — a whistle.*

Find a straw and cut the end so that it makes a point. Flatten the point and put the straw in your mouth and blow.

Cut several straws of different lengths and tape them together. In this way you can make your own "pan pipes."

Find a blade of grass and stretch it between your thumbs. Now blow. The blade of grass makes a harsh sound by vibrating.

Another way of making a flute of sorts is to blow across the top of an empty bottle. Put some water in the bottle and see what difference it makes. You can change the pitch of the note by adding more or less water.

MUSICAL MASTER

Once, at a concert, a pianist found that the screw of his piano stool had been overgreased. All of a sudden he found himself facing the wrong way, away from the keyboard. But this wasn't all. After a few moments the keys started to stick. He tried to release them by kicking the piano, and a leg fell off.

He became so upset that he had to be dragged off the stage when he attempted to use an ax on the piano.

TISSUE BOX GUITAR

Collect a supply of long rubber bands. Make sure that they are of different thicknesses. Find an empty tissue box, one with a hole in it as shown.
1. Cut two pieces of balsa wood to match the shapes in the picture.*
2. Glue the balsa-wood pieces firmly onto the tissue box.
3. Fit the rubber bands around the tacks. You may need to strengthen the box by fitting some wood at the ends.

Try out rubber bands of different thicknesses.

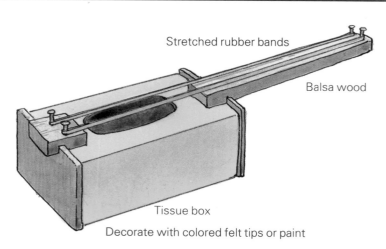

Stretched rubber bands

Balsa wood

Tissue box

Decorate with colored felt tips or paint

*Ask an adult to help you.

TWANGERS

You can make a brick twanger by stretching your rubber bands around a brick.

Make a selection of instruments using different boxes. If you can find a piece of wood, knock in some nails and stretch out a rubber band between two of them. What kind of sounds can you make now?

Try making a set of twangers with high and low notes.

A really deep sound can be made using an old plastic bucket or dishpan. Turn this upside down and attach a stick or cane to the side. You could use lots of cellophane tape for this. Make a hole in the dishpan. Tie a knot in the string, push it through the hole and stretch

it to the top of the cane. Attach it firmly and twang away.

SHAKE IT

Find two used yogurt containers, wash them and put ten dried beans in one of them. Join the containers with cellophane tape and shake away. What happens if you add more beans or use something else in your shaker, such as rice?

Tape

Yogurt container

You could try different containers — for example, an empty plastic juice bottle or an empty dishwashing-liquid container.

THE BAND

Well, this is it. Get together some friends and your instruments. Divide your band up into a wind section, which should include the bottles and flutes and maybe a clean comb with paper. Next make up a string section with the twangers and the guitars. The

percussion should include the shakers and some bangers such as cookie tins turned upside down, or maybe cardboard boxes.

You may be able to add to this list with a few sounds made with your hands or feet.

Take it away, gang!

SECRET MESSAGES

There are a number of ways to send a message to a friend without anyone else knowing about it. The safest method is to develop a code between the two of you. Then, if the message ever went to the wrong person, that person would have to break your code before he or she could understand your message. Here are some ideas.

CODES AND CIPHERS

Ciphers and codes have been used for centuries to send messages. There are many different methods of devising a code, including using numbers and symbols. One of the simplest codes is this one:

A = 1   B = 2   C = 3   D = 4
E = 5   F = 6 ...

Each letter of the alphabet has a number. This code uses a sequence of numbers and would be easy to crack. Try thinking up more complex codes using numbers. Another way of producing an alphabet code is to reverse the letters of the alphabet, for example: A = Z

B = Y   C = X   D = W   E = V
F = U   G = T   H = S ...

This would be quite easy to crack on its own. To make it trickier, try the three-letter code. This was used in World War II. Start by reversing the letters of the alphabet so that A = Z, B = Y and so on. But when you write your coded message this time, do not write in sentences but only in groups of three letters. Don't worry if you have one or two letters left over at the end, just add Xs and Os. Try decoding this: NVV GNV GLM RTS GXO.

AMAZING MONOPOLY

Monopoly was first sold in 1935, and it is estimated that it is now played by over 250 million people worldwide.

One of the best stories about Monopoly concerns prison camps in World War II. A secret British department made up silk maps that were slipped into the backs of Monopoly boards. These showed escape routes from the particular prison to which the game was sent. The Monopoly money was also replaced by the real money of the country in which the prison was situated. So this was one way of getting secret messages into prisons.

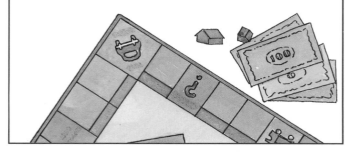

LEMON INK

Dip a matchstick into some squeezed lemon juice, and then write a message on a piece of clean white paper. Allow the juice to dry and watch the message disappear.

Now heat the paper gently over a lightbulb or in the oven and watch it mysteriously reappear. *

*Ask an adult to help you.

THE WAXY WAY

Rub a candle over a piece of paper and put the waxed side facedown on another sheet of paper. Write your message on the back of the waxed sheet, pressing down hard. Sprinkle some poster-paint powder onto the second sheet and give it a good shake.

TREASURE TROVE

Draw your own treasure map, and make up some clues using your invisible writing or a code. Give the clues to a friend, and see if he or she can work out where the treasure is hidden. Put some interesting features onto your map to try to confuse anyone who finds the map.

WET AND DRY

Wet a sheet of paper without making it too soggy. Press a piece of dry paper on top. Write your message on the dry paper. If you hold the wet paper up to the light, your message will appear. When the paper dries out, the message disappears, but if you wet it again, it comes back.

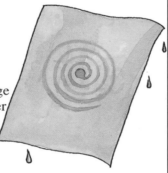

SECRET WRITING

Think of as many different uses as you can for your secret writing. You could start a secret club that uses a special code, or you could write in a diary in invisible ink so that no one can read what you have written.

MORSE CODE

One of the most famous invisible codes was invented by Samuel Morse. This code is heard rather than seen and is used by ships to communicate with one another. It is an international code that sends messages by wire or radio using a series of short dots and long dashes. It was first introduced in 1838. It is now used less often than before because of the development of new technology.

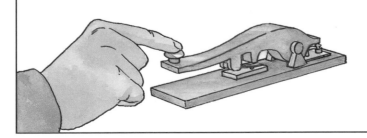

A ● ▬	N ▬ ●
B ▬ ● ● ●	O ▬ ▬ ▬
C ▬ ● ▬ ●	P ● ▬ ▬ ●
D ▬ ● ●	Q ▬ ▬ ● ▬
E ●	R ● ▬ ●
F ● ● ▬ ●	S ● ● ●
G ▬ ▬ ●	T ▬
H ● ● ● ●	U ● ● ▬
I ● ●	V ● ● ● ▬
J ● ▬ ▬ ▬	W ● ▬ ▬
K ▬ ● ▬	X ▬ ● ● ▬
L ● ▬ ● ●	Y ▬ ● ▬ ▬
M ▬ ▬	Z ▬ ▬ ● ●

MORE CODES

Down in the darkness of a secret bunker sit the expert code breakers. Their job is to crack the most difficult codes in the world. Can you devise a code they cannot break?

There are also many different codes that are recognized all over the world. International codes allow people to communicate and send messages over great distances.

MORE CODES

Some codes are simple and straightforward to use while others are extremely difficult to crack. Codes are used by a variety of people. For example, the police have a code that they use to be certain of a message. It spells out the letters of the alphabet: A–Alpha, B–Bravo, C–Charlie, D–Delta. This code is also used by airline pilots.

Another code is Braille, which is a special code used by the blind. It uses a series of raised dots that represent numbers and the letters of the alphabet and are read by touch. It was invented in 1829 by Louis Braille, who had been blind from the age of three. Books and magazines are produced in Braille, using machines.

Semaphore is a type of code that uses two markers or flags. Each letter and number is represented by changing the position of the markers or flags.

USING PICTURES

Here are some codes that have been made up using pictures and words. See if you can work them out:

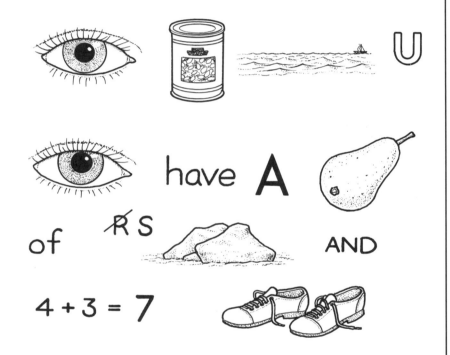

CRYPTIC CLUES

Here is a code that uses numbers instead of letters. See if you can work out what these coded messages mean.

14.38.36.16. 36.16.
20.12.36.14.44. 44.52.16.4.

28.36.26.46.50.44.26.46.44.18.16.

Using this system, make up some of your own messages and give them to a friend to decode. Make sure that you give him or her the code breaker, unless you want to make your friend crack it without any help at all.

A = 52 B = 50 C = 48 D = 46
A B C D E F G H I J K L M N O P Q R S T U V W X Y Z
52 50 48 46 44 42 40 38 36 34 32 30 28 26 24 22 20 18 16 14 12 10 8 6 4 2

USING SYMBOLS

Julius Caesar was away from home much of the time on campaigns to quell uprisings in the farther reaches of his empire. He needed to keep in touch with home but did not want to write publicly, so he invented a code.

His code was not very complicated. It was a displacement code, and it worked like this. He wrote down the alphabet, then underneath wrote the third letter further on in the alphabet, like this:

ABCDEFGHIJKLMNOPQRSTUVWXYZ
DEFGHIJKLMNOPQRSTUVWXYZABC

To put a letter into code, he wrote down the message but used the lower alphabet. If the message was "We won again" he would have written

ZH ZRQ DJDLQ

(The Roman alphabet does not contain the letters J, K, W and Y, but the code is more useful with these letters.)

This code is easy to break, because the letters are still grouped as before. And the pattern can easily be spotted, as A will always be D, B will always be E etc.

This substitution code was invented by an Italian named Giovanni Baptista della Porta. It gets around the problem of letters always coming out the same. He wrote the alphabet four different ways and gave each a number.

1. A B C D E F G H I J K L M
   N O P Q R S T U V W X Y Z

2. A C E G I K M O Q S U W Y
   B D F H J L N P R T V X Z

3. M L K J I H G F E D C B A
   Z P R T V X O Y W U S Q N

4. M S I Q G R P E O C N A
   T L U J V H W F X D Y B Z

To use the code, write down your message. Take the first word and write down the letter above or below each letter in the first alphabet. Do the same for the second word, but use the second alphabet. Use the third for the third word and the fourth for the fourth, then start again with the fifth word, and so on.

HELPFUL CODES

See if you can find out how the other letters of the alphabet are represented in these codes:

Sign Language.   Semaphore Code.

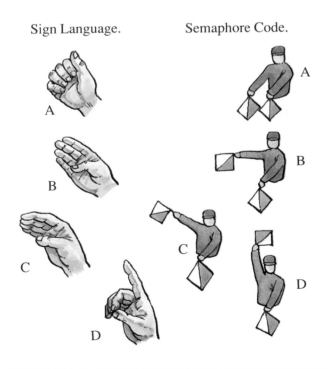

This is called the binary code and it is used by computers. It only uses the numerals 0 and 1, to represent the amount of units, twos, or multiples of two, needed to make a number. The number 1 is made of one in the "units" column. The number 2 is made of one in the "twos" column and zero in the "units" column. The number 7 needs one in the "fours" column, one in the "twos" column, and one in the "units" column.

16	8 4 2 1		16	8 4 2 1
1 = 0	0 0 0 1		6 = 0	0 1 1 0
2 = 0	0 0 1 0		7 = 0	0 1 1 1
3 = 0	0 0 1 1		8 = 0	1 0 0 0
4 = 0	0 1 0 0		9 = 0	1 0 0 1
5 = 0	0 1 0 1		10 = 0	1 0 1 0

Now work your way up to 100.

PICTURE PUZZLES

Here is a mixture of things to blow your mind, from a picture with a difference to the circle of coins, a very old puzzle. Why not try making up two of your own pictures? Make them as similar as possible. Then make some tiny differences. Can any of your friends spot the differences? The puzzle from six matchstick squares to three matchstick squares can be done! Just take your time and think about it very carefully.

ODD MAN OUT

Which one doesn't fit in each sequence?

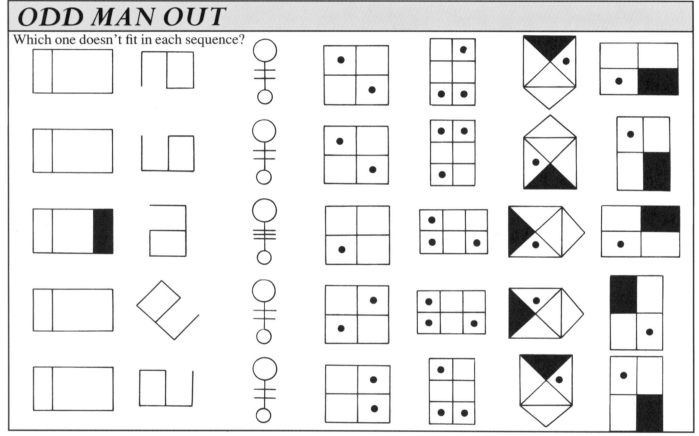

THREE SQUARE

Find fifteen matches and make up the six squares shown below. Now turn the six squares into three squares by removing three matches. It can be done!

ABOUT FACE

Drawing faces is easy when you think about it. Make copies of the faces below. Look carefully at them. Now close the book and see if you can draw them again. How did you do?

Here is a funny face. Copy it onto a piece of paper and turn it upside down. Now what do you see?

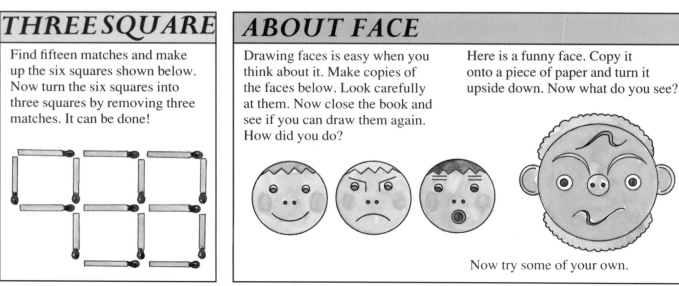

Now try some of your own.

SPOT THE DIFFERENCE

Look at these two pictures and see how many differences you can spot.

PUZZLE

Put six coins of the same type onto a table in the pattern shown. By moving only three of the coins one at a time, can you turn the two lines into a circle?

DOES IT FIT?

Cut out as many tessellations as you can think of (see page 19).* See if you can make up the numbers 1 to 9 using the shapes. You will have to do each one individually.

Using your shapes, now make the following letters:

A   Z   T   M   G

Is it possible to make up all the letters of the alphabet? Try it!

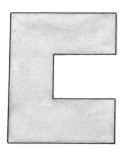

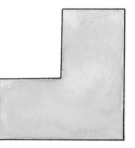

*Ask an adult to help you.

COLORED BOXES

Color is all around us, yet it is not always what it seems. Only three colors — blue, red and yellow — are pure. These three colors are known as the primary colors. All other colors are made up of combinations of colors. Artists use this knowledge in mixing their paints. Some people are color blind. This means that they have a hard time recognizing the differences between certain colors.

THE COLOR OF THE SKY

Have you ever wondered why the sky is blue during the day or why it can sometimes look red at sunset?

As the light from the sun arrives, it is scattered by dust and water particles in the air. The light at the violet end of the spectrum tends to get scattered more than the rest and comes to us from all angles. That is why the sky looks blue rather than yellow or green. In the evening, when the sun is low in the sky, the light travels through more dust particles than in the daytime. This extra dust scatters all the colors except the reds and oranges. We see a red sky.

Now try out some of these color tests:

FILTERS

Collect together various different-colored see-through candy wrappers. Smooth them out and lay them on the table.

Take a red one and look through it. What can you see? Which of the colors are different from normal? Now take a blue wrapper and look through that. Which colors remain the same and which change? Try out other colored papers such as yellow and green ones. Which colors do they block out and which do they change?

Make up a chart showing the color changes using the different colors.

THE COLOR BOX

Find a small cardboard box — a shoebox would be ideal.* Cut a panel in the side of the box and cover it with a large piece of colored see-through plastic or tissue paper. Put a number of different brightly colored objects into the box.

Put the lid back on the box and look at the objects through the side. What can you see now? Keep the same objects in the box but change the piece of plastic or tissue paper for a different color. Do the things in the box change color?

When you look at something green — for example, grass — it reflects all the light from the green part of the spectrum of colors and soaks up all the other colors. That's why it looks green.

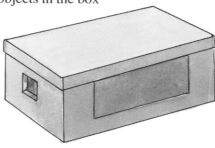

*Ask an adult to help you.

CRAZY GLASSES

Why not make yourself a pair of crazy colored glasses. Get a piece of cardboard and cut out the front.* Cover the lens part of the glasses with a piece of an old colored plastic bag. You could use two colors.

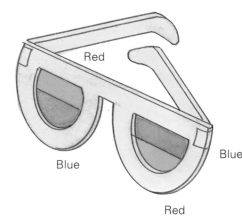

Now decorate your glasses by building up the front. The glasses could have a theme, such as holidays, and be designed like sun umbrellas. If your theme is gardens, then decorate them with plants.

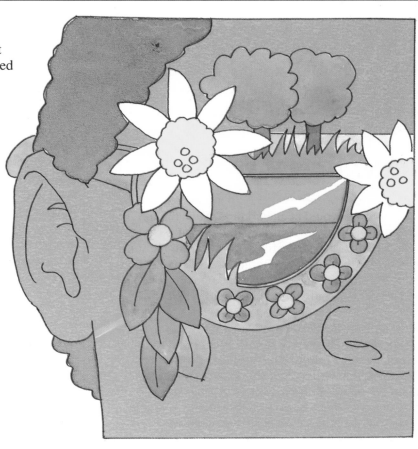

MIXING COLORS

What about mixing colors? There are "warm" and "cold" colors. Warm colors include red and orange; cold colors include blue and green.

Some colors go well with each other while others clash. Try painting one half of a piece of paper red and the other green. What do they look like together? What about purple and yellow?

Colors are used in advertisements to create feelings of warmth and cold. Collect together some advertisements from magazines and see which colors have been used to create different effects.

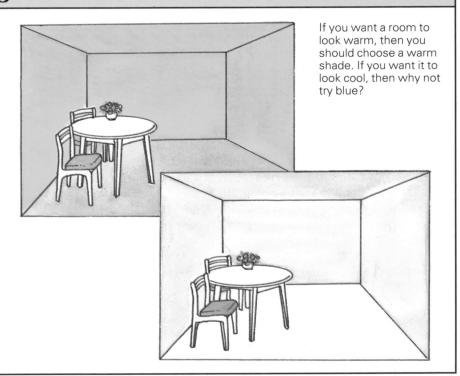

If you want a room to look warm, then you should choose a warm shade. If you want it to look cool, then why not try blue?

*Ask an adult to help you.

LOOKING AT LIGHT

Sometimes things are not as they seem. Leave a jam jar filled with water on a windowsill on a sunny day and you may suddenly find a rainbow on your windowpane. Take a look at your pet fish from the side of its tank, and you may find you have the biggest goldfish in the world. Are these all tricks of light?

SUNLIGHT

Light is a type of energy that is all around us. Without it we would be in darkness. Most things do not actually produce their own light but reflect light from the sun. Powerful light rays from the sun travel to earth across 93 million miles of space. If the sun were to explode, earth would be plunged into darkness in only eight minutes.

Sunlight is made up of different colors, known as the spectrum. The first person to split light into the colors of the spectrum was Isaac Newton in 1665. The device he used to do this is called a prism. A prism is a piece of high-quality glass that is cut in such a way that a beam of light entering one side passes out the other in all its different colors. Newton discovered that light is made up of the colors of the rainbow; red, orange, yellow, green, blue, indigo, and violet.

Today different types of prisms can be used for many things — for optical instruments and cameras and in medicine.

MAGNIFYING GLASS

If you look at a goldfish through the side of its tank, it can look huge. This is because the water acts as a lens.

Put a pencil or straw into a glass of water and look at it from the side. Put your finger in the water and instantly it is the size of a giant's!

You could even read a book using the glass of water to magnify the print. Put the glass against the page of a book and see how big you can make the print.

MAKE A RAINBOW

To make a rainbow, put a dish of water on a sunny windowsill. Prop a piece of paper in front of the dish. Find a small mirror and put it into the dish of water. Move your mirror around until you produce a rainbow on your piece of white paper. This happens because the mirror and the water form a prism, which breaks up the white light.

Next time you see a rainbow, take a look at the colors. They will match the colors on the piece of paper above. This is because the water droplets in the air after a rainstorm act as little prisms, splitting the sunlight into its different colors.

OPTICAL ILLUSIONS

Sometimes, if you are driving down a road on a hot day, you will notice that the road surface in front of you starts to shimmer and pools of liquid seem to be forming.

This is an optical illusion.

The sunlight is playing tricks on you.

People in the desert sometimes think they can see trees and lakes in the distance. These optical illusions, or mirages, are caused by the bending of light rays in the heat. People stranded in the desert have often been tricked into thinking that they are only a short distance from water when in fact it is a long way over the horizon.

If you are ever at an airport on a very hot summer's day, you can see mirages. Airplanes appear to be landing in a shimmering pond of water on the runway. It's all a trick of the light, of course!

BENDING LIGHT

In 1621, Willebrord Snell, a Dutch scientist, discovered that when light goes from air into water, strange things happen.

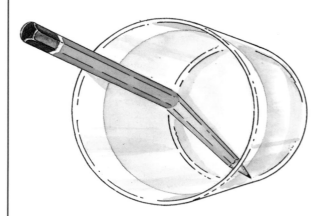

Try this. Put a pencil into a glass of water and look down into the glass. The pencil appears to bend. This is because the light bends as it enters the water.

Put a coin into a bowl. Move back until the coin disappears from view. Now ask someone to pour water into the bowl. The coin comes back into view! This is because the light from the coin bends as the water goes into the bowl.

This effect is known as "refraction."

THE EYE

The eye actually sees things upside down. Your eye projects the image onto a screen at the back of the eyeball called the retina. This then sends messages to your brain along the optic nerve. Information is taken in by the brain and images are perceived right side up.

If you go into a darkened room, the black center part of your eye, called the pupil, increases in size. This is because it is opening up to let in more light. Go out into the light and it closes up again.

Some animals have specialized eyes that can see much better than

ours when it gets dark. This is to gather what little light there is available.

Insect eyes are actually made up of thousands of minute eyes. This helps them to see danger and move quickly. Remember this the next time you try to swat a fly!

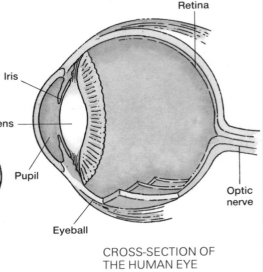

CROSS-SECTION OF THE HUMAN EYE

HEAT IT UP

All matter, whether it is in the form of a liquid, gas or solid, is made up of tiny particles called atoms. When atoms are joined with other atoms, they are known as molecules. No one has ever seen an atom. Scientists use models to show what they think atoms look like and how atoms and molecules behave. Read on about atoms.

HEAT

When atoms and molecules are heated up, they vibrate. As the temperature rises, they bump against one another, faster and faster, creating even more heat, or energy. This energy is

measured in joules, named after the scientist James Joule. He discovered how to measure the amounts of energy released from the vibrating molecules in many different substances as they were being heated up.

Friction also causes molecules to vibrate. Rub your hands together quickly. Can you feel the heat released by the friction?

CHANGES

As the temperature of a liquid falls, the molecules inside slow down. If they slow down enough they will form regular groups, and the liquid will become solid. If you put a tray of ice cubes in a warm room, the molecules begin to vibrate faster.

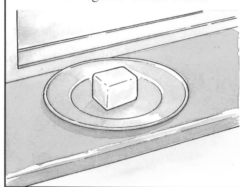

The ice will start to melt and become a liquid again.

If you leave this water on a sunny windowsill for a few days, it will eventually disappear. As the molecules warm up, they vibrate faster and faster, until they break away and begin escaping from the liquid in the form of a gas, called vapor. This change from liquid to gas is known as evaporation.

If this vapor is trapped — under a lid, for instance — the molecules slow down again and return to their liquid form. This is known as condensation.

MOVING AIR

Hot air rises. You can test this out with this experiment.

Take a piece of stiff paper and cut out a spiral as shown in this picture.* Decorate the spiral and fix a piece of cord to the top. Hang the spiral by the cord and check that it is free to move.

Hold it above a warm radiator and watch what happens. As the warm air rises from the radiator, the currents make the spiral turn around.

See if you can make other mobiles that will move in currents of warm air.

Cord

Paper

Radiator

*Ask an adult to help you.

HOW HOT?

Here's how to make your own thermometer: Find a small bottle, some modeling clay, a straw and some colored liquid. Fill the bottle with the colored liquid until it is a third full. Push the straw into the liquid and seal the top with the modeling clay. Make sure that the straw is not touching the bottom of the container. Push the modeling clay down until the colored liquid in the straw is two inches above the top of the bottle. The air inside the bottle expands as the temperature rises and forces the liquid up the straw.

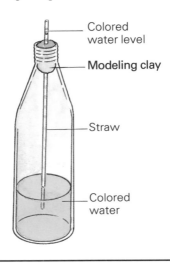

Colored water level

Modeling clay

Straw

Colored water

HOT AND COLD

Some places in the world, such as Death Valley, in California, can be extremely hot, while others, such as Siberia, in the U.S.S.R. can be very cold. The highest recorded temperature in Death Valley was more than 133°F. Siberia can have mild summers, but in winter the temperature has been known to drop to −58°F.

In Finland, where the temperature can fall well below freezing, the cars are fitted with special heaters so that the engines can be kept warm at night. People also have several layers of glass in their windows to keep in the warmth.

KEEPING WARM

In cold weather people often wear woolen clothes. Wool traps warm air between its strands. It is a bad conductor of heat and so prevents your body heat from being lost.

Thermoses are designed to keep liquids hot or cold. The thermos has two walls made of glass. The air is taken out from between these walls, producing a vacuum across which heat cannot travel. Double glazing is another way of keeping the heat in. The heat is unable to escape through the window because of the trapped air between the layers of glass.
Find three containers and a different material to cover each one — for example, wool, cotton and polystyrene. Half fill each container with hot water. Cover them completely. Leave the containers for a few minutes. Which cover is the best insulator, and which container has cooled the quickest?

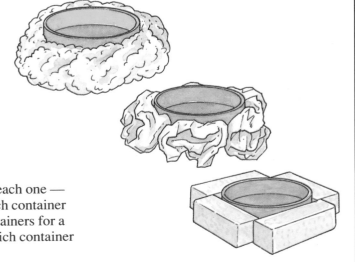

WATER, WATER

Water is all around us. All life on earth, whether it is animal or plant, needs water to survive. Water, being liquid, has many unusual properties. For example, why do some objects float and others sink? How can the insect called a water strider "walk" across the water? These questions seem difficult at first sight, but when you know *why* these things happen, the answers seem simple. Have a look below!

EUREKA!

Archimedes had been called to meet with the king the night before his bath. The king was worried because he thought that the maker of his crown had not used pure gold. He asked Archimedes to work out whether or not the crown was pure gold. Archimedes worked out that if the king's crown displaced exactly the same weight of water as an object of the same weight that was known to be pure gold, then the crown would be pure gold as well. He found that the crown displaced a greater weight of water than the block of pure gold, and so must have been adulterated with a cheaper, less dense metal. It was this problem that Archimedes was thinking about when he stepped into his bath.

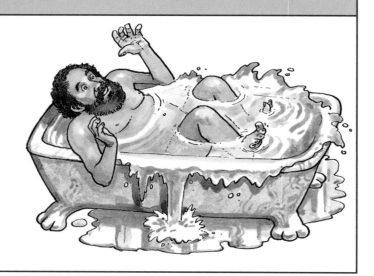

FRUITY FLOATERS

Baffle your friends with this water puzzle. Take an orange and put it into the water. It floats. Now peel the orange and watch what happens when you put it into the water this time. It should sink. Remember, experiments don't always work, so don't be surprised if your orange doesn't sink. Just try it again.

Now try it with some other types of fruit. Does an apple sink when you peel it, or a banana when you take off the skin? Will a tomato sink?

A TOUCH OF GOLD

Archimedes had been called to meet with the king the night before his bath. The king was worried because he thought that the maker of his crown had not used pure gold. He asked Archimedes to work out whether or not the crown was pure gold. Archimedes worked out that if the king's crown displaced exactly the same weight of water as an object of the same weight that was known to be pure gold, then the crown would be pure gold as well. He found that the crown displaced a greater weight of water than the block of pure gold, and so must have been adulterated with a cheaper, less dense metal. It was this

problem that Archimedes was thinking about when he stepped into his bath.

Science

WATER STRIDERS

There are some creatures that can run over the surface of water. One of these is called the water strider. It uses the surface tension of the water to stop it from sinking. The surface of the water is like a skin. This "skin" on top of the water bends beneath the strider's legs but does not break. Take a look the next time you go to your local pond, and you might spot some water striders.

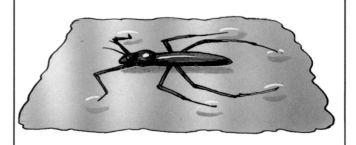

TEST IT OUT

You can test Archimedes' principle by filling a small container to the brim with water. Push a small block of wood down into the water. The amount of water that is lost is the same volume as the piece of wood. Refill the container using a measuring cup and see just how much water was lost. The relationship of the weight of the wood to the weight of the water displaced will indicate the density of the wood.

FLOATERS AND SINKERS

Collect a number of small objects, and fill a bucket halfway with water. See which of the objects float and which sink.

DID YOU KNOW?

Did you know that if you fill a glass with water it is possible to float a needle on the surface? The easiest way is to put the needle on a small piece of paper towel. Once the towel has soaked up the water it will sink, leaving the needle floating on the surface. Pierce the "skin" of the water and the needle will sink.

PROBLEM POSER

Why does a boat float?

TIME

Traveling around the world, you pass through different time zones. When it is lunchtime in the eastern United States, it is evening in England, nighttime in India and early morning in eastern Australia! Some countries are so vast that they cover several time zones.

OLD TIME?

If you look in a dictionary under the word "time," you will see that it is defined as the passing of minutes, hours, days, months and years.

Many years ago people measured time by putting a stick in the ground and watching the shadow cast by the sun move. It was in 1581 that Galileo discovered that time could be measured by using a pendulum. A pendulum is a weight at the end of a string or stick. The weight swings back and forth in a rhythmic motion. The distance between the two points the weight travels with each swing is called the period. This regular motion can be used to measure time. Clocks are one way of measuring time. The earliest date back to the Chinese, who were using them 1,400 years ago.

About 3,000 years ago people in Babylon worked out how long it took the earth to go around the sun. This worked out at 365 days, 6 hours, 15 minutes and 4 seconds. Modern calculations show that those figures are only about half an hour off.

WHAT'S IN A DAY?

A day lasts 24 hours. There are 1,440 minutes in a day and 86,400 seconds.

Years ago people measured the day from sunrise to sunset.

If you go on a long airplane journey from west to east or east to west, your day could be really confusing.

When you travel east or west around the world, you go through different time zones. If you go west faster than the earth revolves, then you will go back in time, as we measure it. If you go east, then you will go forward in time. The world is divided into 24 time zones. When it is 12 noon in Greenwich, London, the time in New York is 7 A.M. In Finland it is 2 P.M. In China it is 8 P.M. This means you have to put your watch forward when you fly east, and backward when you fly west.

Time zones were first used in 1884, when a line through Greenwich Observatory in London was chosen as the starting point for all time zones. This was called the prime meridian.

On the other side of the world from Greenwich lies the International Date Line. Someone crossing this line from east to west loses a whole day, and crossing from west to east gains a day. So if you stood on a Pacific island one Monday on the west of the line and quickly moved east to the next island it would suddenly be Sunday.

ATOMIC CLOCK

In 1966 an atomic clock was built that is accurate to one second in over 1.5 million years. It was built by the U.S. Naval Research Laboratory in Washington, D.C.

MAKING TIME

Sand clocks were used by the Romans. Today, sand timers, or hourglasses, are often used to time a boiled egg.

An hourglass is easy to make. All you need are two empty small bottles and some tape. Fill one of the bottles halfway with sand. Tape the two bottles together. Now turn them over and watch the sand run through. If it runs through too quickly, take your bottles apart and fit in some form of controller, such as a lid with a small hole, so that the flow of sand can be limited. How long does it take for the sand to run through?

Sundials use shadows to tell the time. They will work only when the sun is out. An upright stick will cast a shadow on the ground. As the sun appears to get higher in the sky, the shadow gets shorter. Remember it is the earth that is really moving. See if you can make your own sundial.

Water clocks were first used by the ancient Egyptians around 3,500 years ago. You can make one with a bottle, a yogurt container and a straw with a scale drawn on it, as shown at right. The water trickles through a hole in the bottom of the yogurt container and into the bottle. By watching the water rise up the scale you can tell how much time has passed.

DIGITAL TIME

What kind of watch do you have? A digital one or one with hands?

An ordinary watch has two hands and numbers on the face. The hands are turned by a driving wheel which is adjusted to rotate once every hour. This drives the minute hand. The other hand is driven through two gears which slow it down.

Digital watches are different from ordinary watches, as they do not have hands and a face, but a digital display instead. At the center of a digital watch is a quartz crystal which vibrates all the time. Each time there is a vibration it releases an electric signal. The microchip counts the signals produced by the crystal and regularly sends a signal to the display to change the numbers.

TIME AND SPACE

If you lived on other planets in the solar system your days would be completely different from those on earth. Planets farther away from the sun have much longer years, while those nearer the sun have much shorter years. A year on Uranus is 84 Earth years. That means that if you could live on Uranus you would only have, at the most, one birthday in your whole lifetime. The length of day on each planet depends on how long it takes for it to rotate. On Earth it is 24 hours, and on Mercury it is 59 earth days.

1. Mercury 2. Venus 3. Earth 4. Mars 5. Jupiter

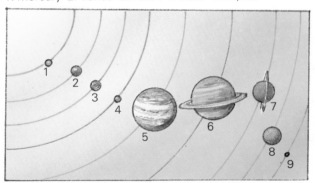

6. Saturn 7. Uranus 8. Neptune 9. Pluto

MIRROR, MIRROR

"Mirror, mirror, on the wall, who is the fairest of them all?"

Here are two pages of magical mirror tricks for you to try. You can write mirror messages, make your own mirror and look at mirror images in nature. Can you think of any more tricks with mirrors?

MAGIC LETTERS

There are eleven letters of the alphabet that have a vertical line of symmetry and nine that have a horizontal line.

Vertical: Y W T V X M O I A H U

Horizontal: X O K H I C B D E

Put a mirror down the middle of any letter in the first list and the letter will still look like itself. Put a mirror horizontally along the middle of any letter in the second list and the same thing will happen.

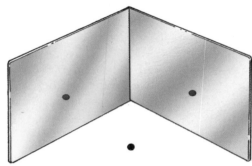

Try out the same idea, but this time use two mirrors joined together as shown.

Are the images any different?

MIRROR WRITING

Mirror writing can be fun. Make up a message and write it down on a piece of paper. Hold it up against a mirror and copy down what you see. Now give the mirror writing to a friend, and ask him or her to work out what you have said.

See if you can work out what these signs would say if they were the right way around.

LOOK OUT

DANGER

HELP!

Emergency vehicles have mirror writing on them so that you can see what they are when you look in the mirror of your car.

SYMMETRY

Take a piece of paper and draw half a house on it, as shown in the picture. Now hold it up to a mirror and see what you get. Try the same idea using half a face. Other ideas to try include animals, butterflies and flowers.

NATURAL SYMMETRY

"Symmetry" is a word that means one side of something matches the other side. There are lots of examples of symmetry in nature, such as butterflies and some shells. A lot of fruit is symmetrical when you cut through it.

You can make a symmetrical butterfly with some paint and a piece of paper. Fold the piece of paper in two. Open it up and put some splotches of paint on one side. Close the paper again and press down on it. When you open it up, you will find that you have a symmetrical pattern. Try out two or three different colors and patterns.

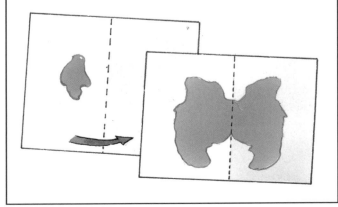

WEIRD REFLECTIONS

Find a large mirror and try putting half your face or body by the side of it. What does it look like?

Take a spoon and look into the bowl. Now turn it over and look at your reflection on the other

side. When you look into the bowl of the spoon, you are looking into a concave shape; when you look at the other side, it is convex.

If you hold a small mirror in front of a larger mirror, you can make the reflections bounce backward and forward to infinity.

See if you can make your own mirror out of aluminum foil.

MAKE IT STICK

Magnets can be great fun to use. There are many different games you can make up using a magnet and a few odds and ends. Magnets are also very useful for everyday purposes; if you look around, you will probably find magnets in different places throughout the house. A compass uses the earth's magnetic field to point north. Read here about how to make your own compass, and try these experiments with magnets.

MAGNETS

Magnets have two poles. One is north and the other is south. If you bring two magnets together, you will find that a north pole always attracts a south and that a north will always repel a north. A south will repel a south but attract a north. The force of a magnet is still not fully understood by scientists.

The earth has lines of magnetic force running through it from north to south. This field of force cannot be seen. Put a piece of paper over a magnet. Then sprinkle some iron filings onto the paper and watch what happens. Now try the same thing using two magnets. By moving the magnets around, you can change the patterns in the iron filings.

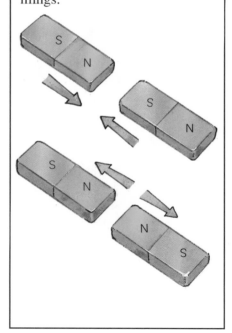

MAKE AN ELECTROMAGNET

Electromagnets are used in junkyards for moving cars and crushed metal. Small electromagnets are also used in hospitals for removing tiny metal splinters from wounds.

To make your own electromagnet, you will need a 4.5-volt battery, some insulated wire and an iron nail.*

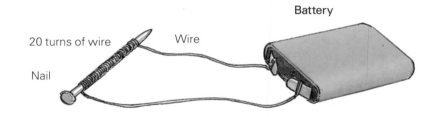

Battery

20 turns of wire

Wire

Nail

Attach one end of the wire to the battery and twist it several times around the nail. See how many pins you can pick up with your magnet. If you increase the turns in the wire, does it make your electromagnet more or less powerful?

If you disconnect one of the terminals, your magnet will stop working.

TESTING OUT YOUR MAGNET

If you have a magnet, you might want to test it to find out how strong it is. This can be done in a number of ways. One is to use pins. Put one pin on the end of the magnet and see how many more pins will stick onto it. The other way is to use paper clips and stick them on end to end. If you have two or three magnets, you can test which is the strongest.

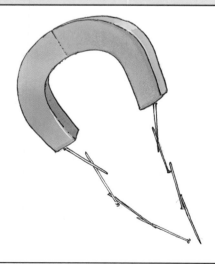

*Ask an adult to help you.

THE MAGNETIC GAME

For this you will need a bar magnet, a length of cord, a long stick, some tape, some cardboard and some paper clips.

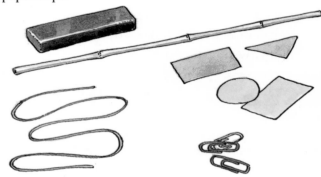

Cut your cardboard into different shapes, such as a square, a circle, a hexagon, an oval.*

Fasten a paper clip onto the back of each shape with a piece of tape. Number each of the shapes.

Paper clip

Cardboard

Now attach the cord to your long stick and tie the magnet onto the other end. Scatter the cardboard shapes on the floor. See which ones you can pick up with your fishing rod. You could make it even more difficult by blindfolding people before they go fishing.

The winner is the one with the highest number of points at the end of the game.

MAKE A COMPASS

A compass is a device for finding your way. Using the earth's magnetic field, a compass always points to the north. It has been used for centuries by sailors to navigate across seas and oceans.

You can make your own compass by stroking a needle one way with a magnet.* Do this about 25 times. Make sure you do not hurt yourself with the needle. Cut a groove in a slice of cork and lay the needle carefully in the groove. Put the compass in a tray of water and watch what happens. The compass should move around and eventually come to rest lying north–south.

Does the compass become more powerful the more you stroke it with a magnet?

MAGNETIC SPIN-OFFS

Magnets can be used to operate automatic switches. These are very useful, especially in burglar alarms. Often these work by a switch that contains a movable magnet. The switch is set into a door frame and lines up with another magnet in the door. When the door is closed the magnet in the switch is pulled forward by the magnet in the door, turning the switch to the "off" position. If the door is opened the magnet in the switch falls back and turns the switch on, activating the alarm.

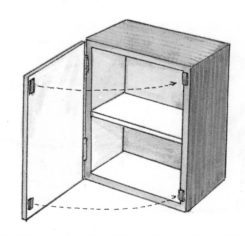

PHONEBUSTERS

Wherever you are, you can keep in touch. Trains, cars and boats all have phones. There are even phones on planes. If you are going to be late, you can phone your friends at your destination to warn them. Be your own phone buff by trying out the projects below.

PHONE FACTS

The telephone of today is very different from that of a few years ago. Telephones no longer have to be connected by wires to the telephone system but can operate independently by using the airwaves. This is how car phones and other wireless phones work. It is now also possible to link phones with computer terminals and video systems.

Videophones carry not only sound but pictures. Older telephone systems relied on thick cables to carry sounds as electrical impulses throughout the network.

Today messages are sent through fiber optic cables. These use tiny pulses of laser light instead of electrical impulses. Laser light pulses can carry a much greater quantity of information more quickly than electricity. Because so much more information is needed to carry a picture than to carry a sound, fiber optic cables are the only way the videophone has become feasible.

A. BELL

People have been sending messages to each other for centuries using flags, smoke and signs. The telephone was invented in 1876 by Alexander Graham Bell, an American

scientist. He later also worked on ideas for a gramophone and undercarriages for airplanes.

Bell's telephone looked different from some of the telephones of today, but the way it worked did not change for many years. He used a thin metal plate called a diaphragm, which vibrated from the sound waves created by someone speaking. These vibrations were turned into a variable electric current by an electromagnet. This traveled down an iron wire to another phone, where the electric current was turned back into sound waves.

HOSEPIPE PHONE

It is easy to make your own simple telephone, so that you can keep in touch with your friends.

Find a length of garden hose. Push a funnel into both ends and then stretch it out. Ask a friend to stand at one end and listen. Speak into the funnel at the other end. Send a message and see if your friend can write it down.

Systems like this were once used in ships and stores to keep in contact.

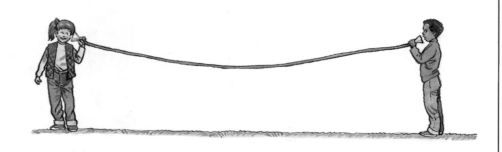

SOUNDS LIKE A GOOD IDEA

Sounds are all around us. Some of them are natural, others are manmade. Make your own list of noises and star the ones that cause "noise pollution" and that could be avoided.

One way to cut down on noise is to insulate. For example, double glazing on windows acts as soundproofing, cutting out a lot of noise. Find an alarm clock and set the alarm to go off in a few minutes. Put the alarm clock into a shoebox and pack it with newspaper. Stand back and wait. How noisy was it? Now try a different type of insulation, such as foam rubber or an old sponge. Are these any better? Which is the best form of insulation you can find?

But back to telephones. Here is a simple phone you can make out of two yogurt containers, some buttons and a long piece of cord or string. Make a hole at the bottom of each yogurt container and thread the string through. Attach it to the button on the inside and pull it tight. Ask a friend to go to the other end of the phone and listen. Send him or her a message. Did it work?

CAN YOU HEAR ME?

Your ears are very delicate parts of your body, and you should always be careful when experimenting with them.

The outer part of your ear collects the sound waves. These waves are sent to the eardrum. This vibrates, and the information passes to three tiny bones. The information finally arrives at the cochlea, which is in the inner ear. This is filled with liquid. The vibrations move the liquid, which, in turn, causes tiny hairs to move. These activate the auditory nerve, which sends a message to the brain.

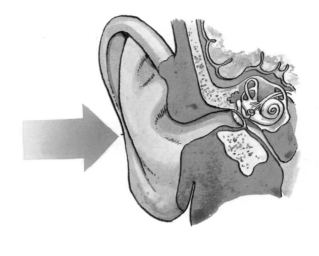

WHAT'S INSIDE?

The first words spoken on Alexander Graham Bell's telephone were "Mr. Watson, come here, I want you." You see, Bell had spilled battery acid all over his trousers.

The modern telephone still works on the same basic principles as Alexander Graham Bell's and the phone shown below. Speaking into the mouthpiece causes tiny granules of carbon that are packed inside it to vibrate. This makes an electrical current flow through the mouthpiece according to the sound waves. Once in the network, conversations are transmitted by pulses of light along fiber optic cables and on to their destinations.

AS FAST AS THAT?

Go into any town and you will see vehicles of all sorts of shapes and sizes traveling at various speeds. How fast can you travel? Do you know the fastest speed of a reptile? How about the slowest speed of a mammal? Have you ever heard of a train that floats? How fast is the speed of light? You can find the answer to all these questions and many more here.

REACTION TIME

Ask a friend to run immediately when you clap your hands. How quickly did he or she move? Ask three or four friends to line up for a race. Get them to run as soon as you blow a whistle. Did you notice a gap between the time you blew the whistle and the moment they started to run? Why do you think this happens?

HOW FAST CAN YOU GO?

If you have taken part in a race, you will know that it takes a lot of energy to run fast. Most people can run at about 12 miles per hour and walk at a speed of 3½ miles per hour.
Set up a test to see how fast you can run. Find an open space and, with a stopwatch, time how long it takes you to cover a certain distance. If you divide the distance by the time it took, you will be able to calculate your speed.

LIGHT SPEED

Light travels at 186,000 miles per second. In one year a beam of light could travel nearly 5,700,000,000,000 miles.

A light-year is the distance that a beam of light will travel in one earth year. The nearest star to earth is 4.3 light-years away. The earth is approximately 93 million miles from the sun. That means that it takes about 8 minutes for light to reach the earth from the sun, but this varies according to the time of year.

PROBLEM

If you lived on a planet where there were 100 hours in every day, 100 minutes in every hour and 100 seconds in every minute, how many seconds would there be in a day?

FAST MOVERS

There are many fast-moving vehicles around today. The TGV is the French high-speed "Train à Grande Vitesse." It can run at speeds of up to 167 miles per hour on specially laid tracks. The network stretches across France and has been in service since 1981.

In Japan a train has been developed that reaches speeds of over 300 miles per hour. This is known as the ML500 and is one of the latest in the "maglev" prototypes. "Maglev" stands for "magnetic levitation." In a maglev system, the train is suspended about 12 inches above an aluminum or copper track. Maglev trains have very strong magnets underneath them that push against other magnets, and lift the train off the track. An electrical current propels the train forward. The train "floats" above the rail while it is running, so there is almost no friction. This allows maglev trains to travel at high speeds. Maglev trains are very light and do not wear out as quickly as other trains.

The Concorde made its fastest crossing between New York and London in 1983, when it took only 2 hours 56 minutes and 35 seconds.

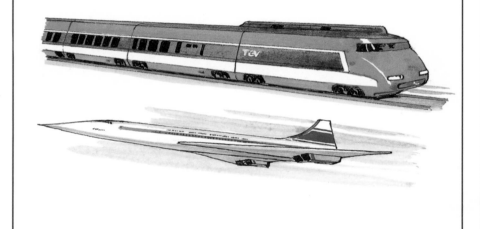

QUICK DRAW

Take a ruler and hold it at the top in your right hand. Let it go and catch it in your left. Easy? Now try using the other hand. What do you notice? Ask someone else to drop it. Now try to catch it. When you let go of the ruler, your brain is ready for it. When someone else does it, there is some delay in your response.

Try dropping the ruler and asking a friend to catch it. Mark on the ruler where you and your friend catch it. Who has the quicker reaction time?

NATURAL SPEED

The fastest speed of a reptile on land is 18 miles per hour. This was for a six-lined racerunner lizard, recorded in the United States. The fastest animal on earth over short distances is the cheetah, which can reach speeds of over 62 miles per hour. Over long distances the pronghorn antelope comes in first, with speeds of 30 miles per hour over distances of 6 miles without tiring.

The slowest mammal is the three-toed sloth of tropical South America. It moves at a speed of about 0.07 miles per hour. This can rise to 0.17 miles per hour when moving in trees.

Cheetah

Sloth

BRAINTEASERS

There are a lot of tricks and puzzles around that are really quite baffling and stump even the cleverest detective. See how you do with these. Some of them are a lot harder than others. When you have finished, list the puzzles in order of difficulty. Ask a friend to try them out and make his or her own list. Are your lists the same?

COIN PUZZLE

This is an impressive puzzler. Ask a friend to take a coin out of his or her pocket and to tell you the third figure in the date on the coin. Now double it. Add 5. Multiply by 5. Add the last figure in the date to the answer. Take 25 away from the total and you will have the year on the coin.

Here is an example: the coin has 1965 on it. The third figure is 6. Double it – that gives you 12. Add 5 – that gives you 17. Multiply by 5 – that gives you 85. Add the last figure on the date, which makes 90. Take away 25, and that gives you 65.

ODD ONES

See if you can spot the odd ones in these lists:

robin thrush sea gull sparrow blackbird
green yellow brown mauve white
London Paris New York Rome Moscow
wine water milk bread tea
mother father son brother sister

MISSING FIGURES

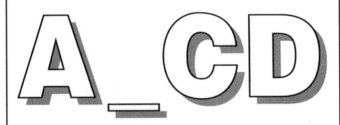

Each of these sums has a number missing. Can you work out what it is?

1. $123 + 345 = 4?8$
2. $?65 + 324 = 589$
3. $678 - 53? = 142$
4. $25 \times ? = 125$
5. $1000 + ? = 2500$
6. $1500 - ? = 100$
7. $20 \times ? = 140$
8. $10 + 10 + ? = 1200$
9. $6 \times ? = 180$
10. $5 + ? + 10 = 25$

FAMILY TREE

What relation is:

1. Mr. Bowles to his son's daughter?
2. Mrs. Jones to her sister's brother?
3. Jill to her brother's wife?
4. Dawn to her mother's brother?
5. Barry to his mother's husband?
6. Peter to his father's father?

LOGIC

Katie and Jessie learn German and French. Jessie and Robert learn French and Italian. John learns Russian and German and Katie also learns Russian.

1. Who learns German but not French?
2. Which language does Jessie not learn?
3. Who learns German, French and Italian?
4. Who learns Russian but not French?

VERTICES

Try to draw the shapes on the right without taking your pencil off the paper and without covering the same line twice. Some are easy and some not. You can work out whether it is possible using the rules a Swiss mathematician called Euler made up over 200 years ago. The points where lines meet are called vertices. Some of these shapes have an odd number of lines meeting, some an even number. Euler worked out that you could draw certain shapes without taking your pencil off the paper, or traverse it, if there were no more than three odd vertices. Any more than this and the figure could not be traversed.

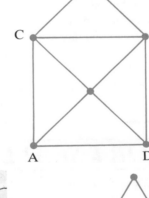

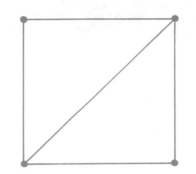

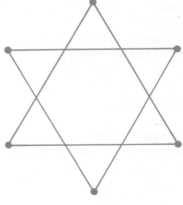

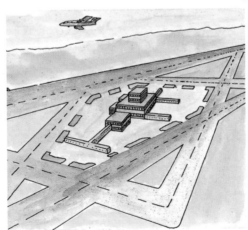

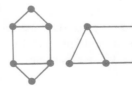

WEATHER MATTERS

Weather patterns differ depending on where you live in the world. In the northern hemisphere, the farther north you go the colder it becomes. In the southern hemisphere, the colder regions are in the south. Some places have a lot of rain, while others are extremely dry. People have always tried to record weather patterns and predict what the weather will be. Read about how to record the weather for yourself.

WEATHER FACTS

There are many traditional weather sayings, for example:

"Red sky at night, sailor's delight; red sky at morning, sailors take warning."

Translated, this means that if you see a red sky at night, then the next day will be fine; if the sky is red in the morning, then the weather will be bad that day.

Another saying is: "If the north wind doth blow, we shall have snow."

There are other signs that, according to country folklore, are supposed to tell us about the weather. If there are berries on the bushes in autumn, then we are likely to have a bad winter; if the cows are sitting down, then it is going to rain.

BEAUFORT SCALE

The Beaufort Scale was invented by Sir Francis Beaufort. It is a scale that shows the strength of the wind and is used by forecasters. It goes from 0 to 12 and was first used to indicate the condition of the sea.

When storms reach force 12 the wind speed is 74 miles or more per hour. These violent storms are called hurricanes, typhoons in the Far East and willy-willies in Australia. They can cause very bad damage, destruction and flooding.

Hurricane Hugo, which hit the Caribbean and much of the Eastern United States in September 1989, was at number 12 on this scale.

FORCE	STRENGTH	SPEED (in mph)	CONDITIONS
0	CALM	less than 1	Sea mirrorlike. Smoke going up straight.
1	LIGHT AIR	1–3	Slight ripples on the sea. Smoke drifting.
2	LIGHT BREEZE	4–7	Wind on face. Leaves moving on trees.
3	GENTLE BREEZE	8–12	Twigs moving.
4	MODERATE BREEZE	13–18	Small branches moving. Waves on sea.
5	FRESH BREEZE	19–24	Shrubs swaying. Quite big waves.
6	STRONG BREEZE	25–31	Big branches moving. Large waves.
7	MODERATE GALE	32–38	Whole trees moving.
8	FRESH GALE	39–46	Twigs and small branches breaking off. Walking difficult.
9	STRONG GALE	47–54	Branches blown down.
10	WHOLE GALE	55–63	Trees uprooted. Damage to buildings.
11	STORM	64–73	Widespread damage.
12	HURRICANE	74 and above	Violent destruction.

SATELLITE HELP

Satellites are used to help forecast the weather. Some of these are "geostationary" and make one orbit in the same amount of time as the earth takes to rotate. Others orbit around the earth taking photographs of the surface. METEOSAT satellites photograph about a quarter of the earth's surface every 30 minutes. Satellites also receive information from weather ships and balloons and relay this to weather centers around the globe.

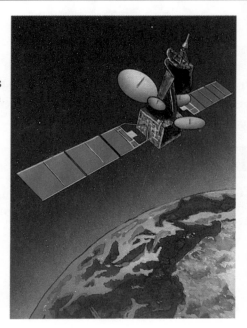

RAIN GAUGE

There are a number of different ways you can record the weather yourself.

See if you can find an outdoor thermometer. Place it somewhere safe outside. Record the temperature at the

Rain gauge

same time every day and keep a graph or chart of your results. This will show you whether the weather is getting warmer or colder.

Another idea is to set up a rain gauge. You can cut the top off a clear plastic 2-liter bottle and turn it upside down to act as a funnel. Use the bottom of the bottle as your rain collector. Mark a scale in inches down the outside. Leave your rain gauge somewhere in the open and check it weekly. This will tell you how much rain there has been.

CLOUDS

Knowing the types of clouds in the sky will help you in your weather forecasting. Cirrus clouds are the feathery ones. The ones that look like puffy cotton balls are called cumulus. The clouds in layers are called stratus. If you see cumulonimbus clouds, it will probably rain, or there may be a thunderstorm. These are usually black or dark gray underneath.

Cirrus

Cumulonimbus

Stratus

WEIRD WEATHER

There has been some weird weather around the world.

Sometimes when it rains in England, the Sahara Desert's sand comes down as fine dust mixed in with the raindrops.

In Italy people fire rockets into the clouds to break up huge hailstones before they fall and damage the crops.

In Alaska in 1971, the temperature dropped to −80°F!

One of the worst accidents with lightning was in 1769 in Brescia, Italy. A bolt of lightning struck 100 tons of gunpowder, which exploded, killing over 3,000 people.

The aurora borealis can be seen in the far north of the

Northern Hemisphere. It is a beautiful display of lights in the night sky. It can usually be seen after an eruption on the surface of the sun called a solar flare, which can be many times larger than the earth.

The aurora borealis is usually seen in the Arctic regions, but it has been seen hundreds of miles south of this area.

WORMS

Why not worm your way into these amazing facts? The next time you are watching a film about a steamy jungle, keep your eye out for leeches! And when you walk on grass, have a good look and see if you can spot any worm casts. They are those tiny piles of dirt you find on the surface of the grass. Happy worm hunting!

WHAT IS A WORM?

If you go out into a garden and dig down a few inches, you may come across an earthworm.
Earthworms' bodies are divided into segments.
Their mouth is at one end, but they don't really have a head. They have no eyes or ears or nose and feel using their skin.

The earthworm has horny bristles along its body except for the ends. These bristles help it when it moves along the ground. They also anchor it to its burrow.

The first worms appeared around 570,000,000 years ago.

WHERE DO WORMS LIVE?

Most earthworms live in burrows under the ground. Using their front end, they force their way through the soil.

They also eat their way through the soil. The soil passes through their bodies and comes out as a cast.

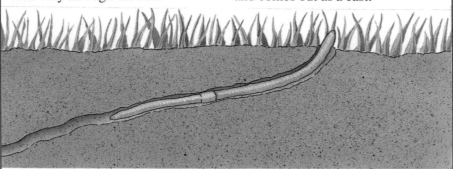

You will also find worms in rivers and in the sea. Tubifex worms live in fresh water and spend their time upside down with their heads in the mud so they can look for food. Their tails stir up the oxygen in the water. This helps their breathing. Lugworms burrow down into the sand and feed by swallowing the sand. This makes a tiny pit at one end of their burrow and a pile of sand at the other.

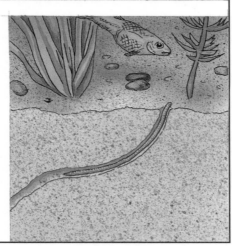

PARASITES

Some worms live inside other creatures and are known as parasites. Tapeworms can sometimes be found inside birds, fish and other animals.

The roundworm is a parasite that can live inside animals as well as human beings. Roundworms are often small and harmless, but they can grow very long.

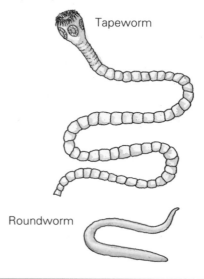

Tapeworm

Roundworm

BUILD A WORM FARM

If you want to study worms more carefully, you will need to build a worm farm. This can be made of two pieces of plastic with wooden ends.

Put in a variety of different soils so you can watch how they burrow and use the soil. The best time of year to look for earthworms is in the autumn. Put some leaves on top of the soil. You can also try feeding them with other things such as pieces of apple. Put your worm farm somewhere cool and dark.

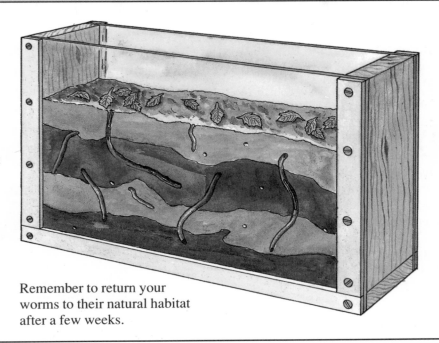

Remember to return your worms to their natural habitat after a few weeks.

SUCKING BLOOD

Leeches were used by doctors many years ago to draw blood. The doctors thought that their patients had too much bad blood in them! Leeches draw blood by piercing the skin of the victim. Some larger varieties can suck the insides out of small creatures such as snails and tiny insects.

WORM FACTS

See if you can get a worm to cross a gap. Put an earthworm on a piece of damp paper towel and put them both on a book. Put a piece of towel on another book and move it a short distance away. Now watch what the worm does. Does it jump the gap?

The heaviest earthworm in the world, called *Rhinodrilus tatner-brazil*, lives in Brazil and can weigh over 10 ounces.

The longest segmented worm ever found measured 22 feet long. It belonged to a group of worms called annelids and was found in the Transvaal, South Africa.

SLOW WORMS

Some worms, such as the slow worm, are not really worms at all. They are in fact lizards without legs. You can tell they are not snakes or worms because they have eyelids. They give birth to live young and eat slugs. They live mostly under stones in damp places and come out in the early evening.

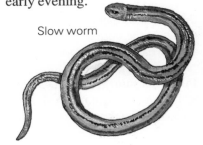

Slow worm

FUN WITH PLANTS

Gardening is a popular pastime in this country. It is hard but enjoyable work, and you don't have to have a large piece of land. In fact, a sunny windowsill is an excellent place to grow seeds. On this page you will find a number of gardening activities. Remember to look after your plants and to give them light and water.

WATCHING THINGS GROW

If you live in a city, you can create your miniature garden in a window box or even inside on a windowsill.

To create a window-box garden, find a good deep box with some form of drainage so that the water can get out. Fill the bottom with some small pebbles or stones, and then fill up your box with some potting soil. Put your box somewhere where there is light and remember to water your plants once they have been put in. The soil should be slightly moist. Why not try a pot geranium or a primrose?

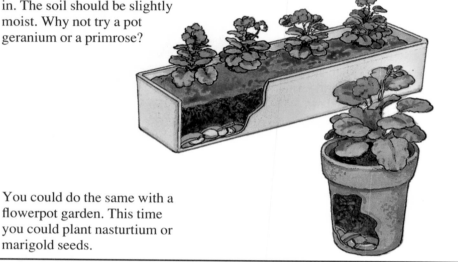

You could do the same with a flowerpot garden. This time you could plant nasturtium or marigold seeds.

LOOKING AT SEEDS

Here are some other ways of growing things.

Slice the top off a carrot and put it into a saucer of water. Place it on a sunny windowsill, keep it wet and watch it grow.

Pineapple tops are also worth growing. Cut off the top of a pineapple, keeping a little of the fruit attached. Allow the pineapple to dry out. When the bottom is dry, scrape it with a knife and put it into a flowerpot that contains damp soil and stones at the bottom. Place a plastic bag over the top of the pot, as shown, to keep it moist. Put it in a sunny place. As soon as the pineapple starts to show signs of growth, remove the bag.

SEEDS

Looking at seeds can be very interesting. One way to study them is to collect a variety of different fruits such as a pear, an apple, an orange and a kiwi. Slice them in half and examine the seeds inside.* How many did you find inside each? Why do you think oranges have a lot more seeds inside than, say, a peach or a plum? Find a piece of paper and draw what you see.

*Ask an adult to help you.

SEED DISPERSAL

There are a number of different ways plants disperse their seeds. For example, ripe cucumbers burst open, spitting seeds everywhere!

Some seeds are spread by the wind. When you blow on a dandelion seedhead the seeds float away. Maple seeds are also spread by the wind.

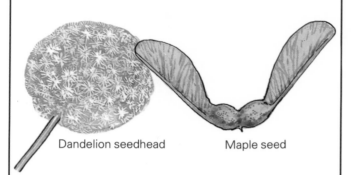

Dandelion seedhead   Maple seed

Some seeds, such as burdock, have tiny hooks attached to them. These get hooked onto the coats of passing animals and drop off elsewhere.

Birds also transport seeds. They eat fruit and then pass the seeds out elsewhere in their droppings.

Burdock

Water also transports seeds. Seeds fall into rivers, streams or the sea and then eventually get washed up somewhere else, where they often take root.

See if you find out any other ways seeds are dispersed.

DID YOU KNOW?

One of the first people to study plants and put them into groups was the Swedish botanist Carolus Linnaeus. He lived between 1707 and 1778. As a child he enjoyed studying plants. He developed the system for classifying animals and plants that is still in use today.

RUNNERS AND RACERS

Growing runner beans using paper towels or wet newspaper can be great fun. Find a jam jar and soak some paper towels or newspaper in water. Cut them up so that they fit inside the jar.* Put a few stones in the bottom of the jar. Slide a few runner bean seeds in between the paper and the side of the jar.

Put it somewhere sunny and warm and watch what happens. If you can locate the growing tip of the seed, then put it in upside down and see if it makes any difference in the way it grows.

Some seeds — such as mustard, watercress and alfalfa — will grow really fast. These can be found at your local health food store. Put some wet paper towels or cotton on a saucer and sprinkle some of the seeds on top. Just watch how quickly they grow. Try some grass seed as well.

When your mustard, watercress or alfalfa has sprouted, trim off the leafy heads as well as the stems and add them to your favorite sandwich or salad.*

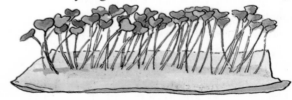

If you were successful growing seeds without soil you might like to try something else. Herbs are easy to grow and are delicious in salads,

sandwiches and sauces. Choose an herb, such as parsley or basil, and plant it in moist soil. Cover the pot with plastic wrap. When the seeds have germinated, take off the plastic wrap and set the pot in a sunny window. Some seeds take longer than others to germinate. When the herbs are big enough, snip off the leaves as you need them.

*Ask an adult to help you.

ALL SHAPES

Take a look at yourself in the mirror. Now look at someone else. Is his or her mouth the same shape as yours? Is his or her hair the same color as yours? We all have differences in the way we look or in our personality type. But no matter what sort of differences there are on the outside, all living beings have many important characteristics in common.

BODY FACTS

Stand next to a friend in front of a mirror. Notice all the differences between you. Everyone is different in some way or other. For example, your eyes or your hair may be a different color from your friend's.

People also have different personalities. Some are naturally quiet, while others are noisy. Some people enjoy reading; others prefer games.

Where people live may also have an influence on what they are like. They may live in the country-side or in a town, at the sea or on a hillside. Wherever people live and whatever they like doing, however, they all have one thing in common: they need energy to keep them going.

Energy is produced from food and also from the oxygen people breathe. It is measured in "calories." The next time you go shopping have a look at the packages on the shelves and you will often spot the number of calories printed on the outside.

One of the most important uses of energy is movement. Some movements are automatic, such as the beating of your heart. Others are produced by commands from your brain to your muscles.

MUSCLE POWER

Your body is full of muscles. Whether you are lying down, sitting or moving, these muscles are working. You have more than 600 muscles in your body.

If you are going to do something strenuous, you have to strengthen your muscles so that they can cope. Marathon runners build up their leg muscles by practicing running, and weight lifters use special weights to increase the power of the muscles in their arms and torso. Ballet dancers have routines to strengthen their leg muscles.

Find a large piece of paper and ask someone to draw around you. Now mark in where you think your main muscles are.

FINGERPRINTS

Your fingerprints are unique to you. No one else has exactly the same patterns on their fingers. Even the fingerprints of identical twins are different. Fingerprints are often used by the police to solve crimes. Officers often dust objects for fingerprints. Once they have these prints they can sometimes match them up with those of someone on their books.

It is quite easy to take your own fingerprints. Find a piece of white paper and some black poster paint. (Make sure the paint is removable.) Paint the tip of one finger and press it lightly onto the paper.

SKELETONS

There are over 200 bones in the adult skeleton. If you break one of your bones, it will usually mend as long it is held together in the right way. As people grow older their bones become more brittle and break more easily.

Inside your bones there is a material called bone marrow. Bone marrow makes new blood cells.

Your skeleton holds your body together. Certain parts of it act as protection. Your brain is covered by your skull, and your heart is protected by your ribs. The 26 bones of the spine, called the vertebrae, protect the nerves that run up and down inside the spine.

Skeletons of animals, fish or human beings that are thousands of years old are sometimes found. These are called fossils. Fossils are formed when bones are buried for a long time under certain conditions. For example, dinosaur bones were often buried under layers of fine mud. Over the years, the mineral content of the bone turned to solid rock. These fossils can often tell us a great deal about life in the past.

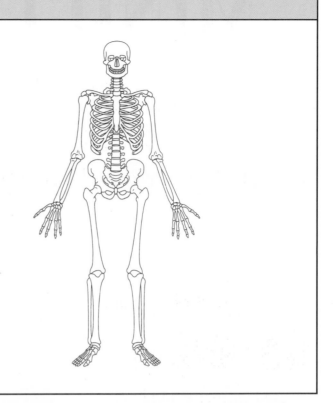

FOOD FACTS

Food is needed for growing, for energy and to keep you healthy. Years ago, sailors at sea did not have fresh fruit or vegetables. This caused scurvy, a nasty illness that made their hair fall out and their gums bleed.

A healthy diet includes a mixture of protein, fat, vitamins, minerals, carbohydrates and fiber. Some foods are high in vitamins, such as oranges and lemons, while others contain a lot of sugar, such as candy. Sugar provides energy, but too much of it rots your teeth.

FOOTPRINTS

How big are your feet?

Take a piece of graph paper and draw around your foot. Now count up the squares. How many have you covered? One way of making sure that you don't count the same square twice is to color the squares in as you count. How big is your foot? Why not make a family or friend foot chart. Who has the biggest and the smallest feet? Now draw around your shoe, and then draw your foot inside the shoe. How well does it fit?

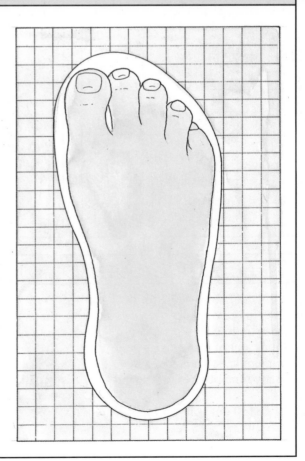

MIND TWISTERS

Here is a mixed bunch of mind twisters to keep you thinking for some time. Some of them are very old. Puzzles have been around for many centuries. There are many stories of how sailors used puzzles and mind twisters to pass the time when they were on long journeys. But you don't have to go away to sea to try these out!

HOW MANY?

Look at these two drawings and see if you can figure out which one contains the most squares.

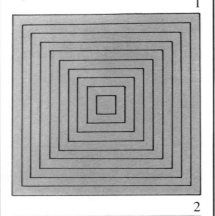

1

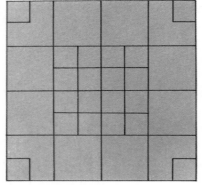

2

HOW MANY SQUARES?

Pauline and Dennis work in a toy factory putting colored balls into boxes. If they have a red ball, a green ball, a yellow ball and a blue ball, how many different ways can they be packed into a box with four sections? The drawing below will help you get started.

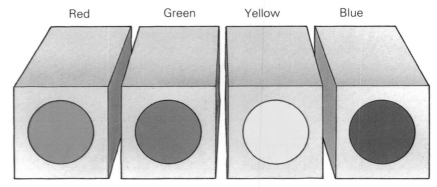

Red   Green   Yellow   Blue

If they were given an extra colored ball and a box with five sections, how many different ways could they pack these?

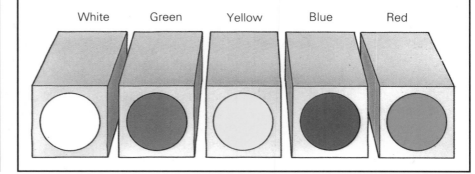

White   Green   Yellow   Blue   Red

THE DICE GAME

You will need one die for this and a piece of paper. Before you start, try to guess how many times, out of ten turns, the die will come down on one, how many times on two and so on.

Then test out your estimate. Was it right?

Try it again, but this time throw the die twenty times. Were your results any better?

Try out this probability test using two dice. Which number will never come up?

ON AND OFF

Brenda drives a local bus. When she leaves the bus station on her journey, she has three people on board. At the first stop she picks up another fifteen people. The next stop is the school. Here she drops off five people and picks up three. At the stop by the factory she picks up another twelve people, but she also drops off four. A train has just gotten in at the station so here she picks up eight people and drops off two.

How many people are on the bus when she pulls into the city bus station, which is the next stop?

Now try this one.

A flight from London to New Zealand leaves with 256 passengers on board. It stops in Geneva and lets off 98 passengers but takes 56 on board. At the next stop, Nairobi, 25 passengers get off and 12 get on. Perth is its next stop, where it lets off 100 passengers. How many passengers are left on the plane when it reaches its final destination at Aukland?

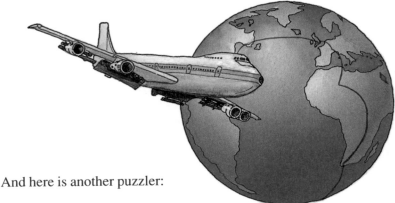

And here is another puzzler:

If there are fifteen crows on a fence and the farmer shoots a third of them, how many are left?

SIX, SEVEN

See how good you are at these – try to do them without using your calculator.

1. $6 \times 6 \times 6 \times 6 \times 6 \times 6 \times 6$

2. $7 \times 7 \times 7 \times 7 \times 7 \times 7$

3. $6 \times 7 \times 6 \times 7$

4. $7777 - 6666$

5. $767,676 - 676,767$

There are sixteen children in a playground. Five of them have six marbles in their pockets, and three of them have seven marbles in their pockets. How many marbles are there in the playground?

PUZZLE

Ask your friend to think of a number. Add nine to the number. Double your answer and add three to it. Now multiply it by three and subtract three from the answer. Divide by six and subtract the first number you thought of. The answer is always ten.

TRICKY ONES

Here are more tricks with matchsticks and some ideas using a ball of string. These are the kinds of puzzles your friends will say cannot be done. But with a little help you will be able to prove them wrong.

Be careful when you are using eggs for your tricks. Try spinning a raw egg and then a hard-boiled egg. Stop them both and then let them go again. Which one keeps spinning?

IT'S NOT POSSIBLE

How can you push an egg into a bottle without breaking it?

With a lot of difficulty? Well, if you know a few tricks, the problem is quite simple. If you try to push the egg in as it is, the shell will break and you will be left with a mess of egg white and yolk.

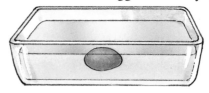

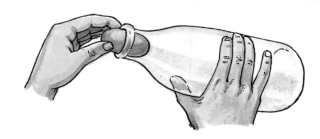

This is how it is done. It is said that Christopher Columbus used to amaze his friends with this scientific experiment.

Take an egg and soak it in vinegar for 24 hours. If it is not soft enough after one day, soak it for 24 hours more.

Now push the egg carefully through the neck of a bottle. Once inside the bottle, the egg will harden again and prove to be a puzzle to all your friends.

UNBREAKABLE EGGS

Another amazing trick is the egg that won't break. Take an egg and press it as shown. However hard you press, it will not break. If you try it any other way, it will crack at once. If there are any tiny cracks in the egg, you might find that it will break, so be very careful and do this trick over the sink, or outside.

Another scientific experiment that might surprise your friends is the floating egg. Put an egg into a container of warm water and then add salt. As more salt is added, the egg will slowly rise to the surface.

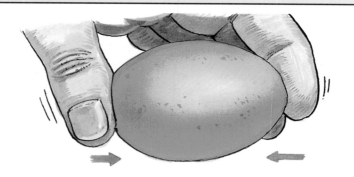

TRICKY TRIANGLES

Look at this triangle and see how many more triangles you can spot inside. Look at the shape of the triangle and see if you can draw one of your own. Start by drawing your triangle and then line AB. Follow this with lines BC and BD. These lines split the sides of the main triangle into two. Now join up DC. Finish off by joining CE and DF.

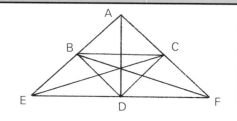

STRINGY ONES

String puzzles can be good fun. Try this one to start with.*

How can you get the string off without letting go of the ends?

Take a pair of scissors and tie a loop, as shown, with a piece of long string. Get a friend to hold the two ends of the string. Take hold of the loop marked X and pull it through the thumbhole on the same side that the two strings pass through. Pass the loop over the points back over the handle of the scissors and slip it off.

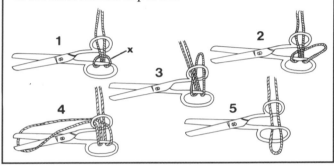

MATCH THESE

Albert Crookfoot had six pigs that he wanted to separate because they were always fighting. He made the pens as shown, using thirteen bits of wood of the same size. When he discovered that one of the pieces was missing, he built the pens with only twelve pieces. Are you as clever as he was?

Here are three triangles. By moving only three matches it is possible to make five triangles. Can you do it?

There are eleven matches here. See if you can sort them out so that they make nine. Impossible?

THE ELECTRIC COMB

If you comb your hair a few times, you should be able to pick up tiny pieces of paper with the comb. It all has to do with static electricity.

The plastic comb becomes charged with static electricity when you run it through your hair, in the same way a balloon will stick to the wall once you have rubbed it against a woolen sweater.

Experiments using static electricity work best on cold, dry days.

See what different kinds of things you can pick up with your comb after running it through your hair. Now test out your friend's hair and see how many tiny pieces of paper you can pick up.

You can also separate salt and pepper using your charged comb. Put a mixture of salt and pepper on a plate. Hold the comb close to the mixture and move it slightly. Watch how the pepper jumps onto the comb and the salt stays still. The pepper moves first because it is much lighter than the salt. Make sure you don't hold the comb too close to the mixture, or you will pick up both!

*Ask an adult to help you.

83

MORE TRICKS

Here is a page of scientific and mindboggling puzzles to baffle and amuse your friends. You can try them out on your own and then show them around. How about doing some of them at your next party and asking people to guess how they work? Once everyone has given up, you can explain how they work. Some of these tricks require skill and quick moves, so be sure and practice before you perform them.

SIGHT LINE

Everything you look at is interpreted by your brain. But sometimes your eyes can play tricks on you.

Try this out. Hold your left forefinger 6 inches out in front of your nose. Now put your right forefinger 1 foot in front of your nose.

What do you see with both eyes open? Close your right eye. What do you see now? Now open your right eye and close your left eye.

Can you work out why this happens? The answer is in the back of the book.

BALANCING TRICKS

Put a piece of paper onto the edge of a glass and balance a quarter on the rim. Now pull the piece of paper away as fast as you can, leaving the coin balanced on the edge of the glass. It can be done!

Now take two Ping-Pong balls, a toilet-paper roll tube, a piece of cardboard and two identical plastic cups.

Cut the toilet-paper roll tube exactly in half. Put the cardboard across the two cups with the tubes on top.

Balance the Ping-Pong balls on the top of the tubes. Now pull the piece of cardboard out from underneath so that the balls fall into the cups.

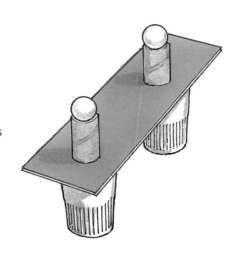

DISAPPEARING AIR

You will need a clear jam jar, a saucer, a candle and a small piece of modeling clay.*

Stick the candle to the saucer with the modeling clay.

Carefully light the candle and put the jar over the top. After a short time something will happen to the candle. Why? Try the same experiment using different-sized containers. How long does the candle burn?

Some fire extinguishers work in this way, by cutting out all the oxygen and smothering the fire.

*Ask an adult to help you.

THE MAGIC HEXAGON

Find a piece of thin cardboard and draw around the hexagon below. Cut out the shape and draw the arrow shown on side one.* Turn the shape over and

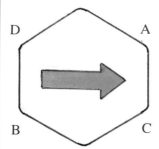

draw an arrow pointing upward on side two. Take hold of the shape between your forefinger and your thumb, making sure that the arrow is pointing to your left.

Hold the shape at point A and B and flip it over to show a friend that the arrow on the other side is pointing in the same direction.

Now turn the card back to its original position. Ask your friend if he or she thinks the arrow will be pointing the same way if you flip the shape over again. They will probably answer yes. Flip it over to show that the arrow has changed direction.

How was it done?

Change the position of your fingers to cover C and D, and the arrow will change position. Once you have mastered this, try holding it so that the arrow points in yet another direction.

FOLDING PAPER

Doing tricks by folding paper is another way to amaze your friends.

In Japan, the art of folding paper into elaborate shapes is called *origami*. In Japanese, *ori* means "a folding" and *gami* comes from *kami*, which means "paper." Simply by folding paper according to ancient rules, delicately shaped flowers and animals can be made.

(i) 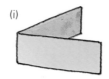   (ii)   (iii)

Cut out a strip of paper (12 inches by 2 inches).* Fold the paper in half and then in half again and again.

(iv)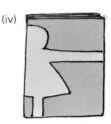

Draw half a person with the arms touching the outside edge and with the head on the folded side.

Cut around the shape — except for the folded side. Now open it up. If it falls apart, try again.

(v)

WATER AND AIR

Do this one over the sink, or a bowl, just in case.

Fill a plastic glass to the brim with water. Slide a piece of cardboard over the top of the glass and turn it upside down. The cardboard should stay where it is. This works because of air pressure.

Put your hand in front of your mouth and blow. What you feel is the air pressing against your hand.

*Ask an adult to help you.

PROBLEM PAGE

Here is a set of problems to set you scratching your head and thinking. They aren't *too* hard, though! Take your time and think them through. The coin puzzle should baffle quite a few people. Make sure you don't give away the solution too quickly. And try to think up some more opposites and problems to try out on your friends.

OPPOSITES

Words are fascinating things, but how much do you know about them? Here are some opposites for you to try out.

Some easy ones:
Hot
Bad
Open
Fat
Small

Now on to some harder ones:

Serious
Dangerous
Expand
Minute
Boring

And finally:

Baby
Nervous
Sober
Tight
Violent

PENTOMINOS

Pentominos can be quite mindblowing.

Take a piece of paper divided into squares, as shown, and draw a shape that uses five squares. This is called a pentomino. You should be able to make up eight different shapes using five squares.

Cut out the eight different shapes you have made and fit them together. See what shapes you can make.

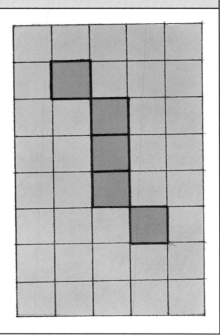

FAMILY PROBLEMS

Try these family problems.

1. A brother and sister were at a party. The man pointed to a boy across the room and said, "That's my nephew." His sister said, "That's not my nephew." Can you sort this out?
2. When I am as old as my brother is now, my sister will be three years older than I am now, and my brother will be twelve years older than my sister is now. If our ages add up to fifty-seven now, how old are we?
3. My father is twenty-one years older than I am. In twelve years, his age will be twice mine. How old am I now?

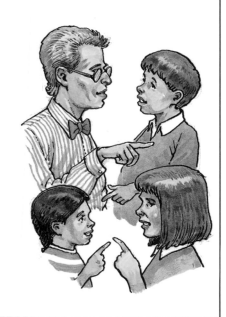

PROBLEMS

If my sister is twenty-one and she is eight years older than I am and my brother is fifteen and he is two years older than I am, how old am I?

Two mothers and two daughters went into a candy store and spent six dollars. If each of them spent the same amount, how much did they each spend?

In four years' time Susie will be twice as old as she was eleven years ago. How old is she?

A plane crashed on the border between Spain and France. In what country did they bury the survivors?

COIN PUZZLES

I have two coins in my pocket that add up to 35¢. One of the coins is not a quarter. What are the two coins?

Put twelve coins on the table so that there are an odd number of coins in every line and you have three straight lines.

Draw this pattern on a piece of paper.

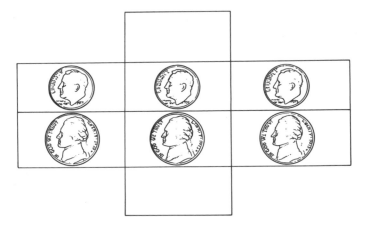

Put three dimes on the top line and three nickels on the bottom.

What you have to do is to move the nickels to where the dimes are in the shape but you can only move one coin at a time. You must move a dime and then a nickel. You can move diagonally, backward, forward or sideways, but only one square at a time, and the square must be empty.

How many moves does it take?

TIME TO STOP

1. If it is 12:47, what will the time be in one hour ten minutes?

2. I catch a train at 6:13, and the journey takes 1 hour 38 minutes. What time do I arrive?

3. I must be at school by 9:00 A.M. If it takes twelve minutes to get there and it is now 8:53, how many minutes late will I be?

4. The clock strikes midnight, and I have been awake for 24 minutes. What time did I wake up?

5. If my bus leaves in 27 minutes and it is now 2:35, what time does it leave?

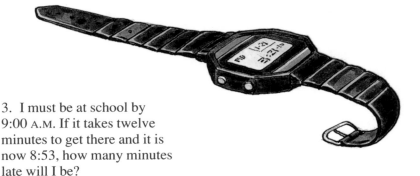

WHAT A CARD!

Long journeys can sometimes be very boring if you do not have anything to do. Or, if you are stuck indoors on a long rainy afternoon, you might find yourself looking for something to do. One good way to spend time is to play cards. Here are some games and tricks you might like to try.

WHO'S THE DONKEY?

This game takes three or more players. If three are playing, you will need two coins or spoons. If there are four players, you will need three coins or spoons. Always have one less coin or spoon than the number of players.

Give each player a piece of paper with the word DONKEY written on it in pencil. Put the pencil in the middle of the table with the coins or spoons.

For three players you will need four queens, four kings and four aces. If there are four players, you will need four jacks, four queens, four kings and four aces.

For each extra player just add the next four cards down in the pack.

The cards are shuffled and dealt facedown so that each person is given four.

The players look at their cards. They take one and place it facedown on the left of them on the table. As this is done, they pick up the card on the right, the one passed on from the person next to them. They must not do this until they have put their card on the table.

The idea is to collect four cards of the same type — for example, four jacks or four aces.

As soon as someone has done this, they put the cards down on the table faceup and pick up one of the coins or spoons. At the same time the other players try to grab one of the other coins. Anyone who fails to pick up something has to draw a line through the first letter of the word DONKEY. The game then starts again. The first person to cross off all the letters is the DONKEY!

A FULL DECK

KING, THREE

Beat Your Neighbor can be played with two or more people. Shuffle the cards and deal them facedown. Do not look at the cards. The player on the left of the dealer starts the game by putting his or her top card faceup in the middle of the table. The next person does the same, putting his or her card on top of the first. This goes on until someone turns up a jack, a queen, a king or an ace. When this happens, the next player has to put down extra cards. For a jack it is one extra card, for a queen it is two, a king is three and for an ace you have to put down four!

If the cards you lay down are all number cards, then the person who laid down the jack, queen, king or ace picks up the whole pile. If you turn over a jack, queen, king or ace, then you stop and the player after you has to put down the correct number of extra cards. If that person has only number cards, then you take the pile. If the person puts down a picture card, then the next player has to put extra cards on top.

The winner of the game is the first person to get all the cards. If you run out of cards during the game, you are out.

YOU CHEAT!

Cheat is played with three or more people, and the idea is to get rid of all your cards.

The cards are dealt face-down. Players pick up their cards. The player to the left of the dealer goes first and places a card facedown on the table, calling out what it is. The next player has to follow with a higher or lower card. If a six is laid down, then the next player has to lay down a five or a seven.

Once the game has started, a player can lay down up to four cards of the same number.

If you do not have the correct cards, you have to cheat. If

another player suspects you, that player shouts "Cheat." If this happens you must turn over the card or cards that you have put down. If you have been cheating, you take all the cards in the pile. If you were not cheating, the other player must take all the cards. The winner of the challenge goes next. If this person wants to, he or she can then start off with a new card. The first person to get rid of all his or her cards wins.

ROYAL TRICKERY

Here is a simple card trick.

Take the kings and two jacks from a pack of cards. Arrange the six cards with the four kings facing you and the two jacks hidden behind the third king. Make sure this is done in private. The audience will see only the four kings. Show the audience the four kings hiding the two jacks. Say that you will now put the four kings on top of the pack. Do this and then take the top card and say that you are now going to move one of the kings. Without showing it to the audience, put it at the bottom of the pack. Now take the next card and put it anywhere and do the same with the next card. Now cut the pack, putting the bottom half on the top. Give the cards to one member of the audience and let the person flick through them. The kings should now be together.

21-CARD TRICK

Take twenty-one cards from the pack. Ask someone to select a card without telling you what it is. Deal the cards into three equal piles, faceup. Ask the person to tell you which pile contains his or her card.

Collect the cards together, making sure that the pile they have pointed to is the second pile you pick up.
Deal the cards into three equal piles. Ask the person to tell you which pile contains his or her card.

Collect the cards together, making sure that the pile containing the card is the second one picked up.

Do this one more time.

Collect the cards and count them out. The eleventh card will be the one chosen.

ANSWERS

pages 12–13
Answer This
1. The coat cost $125, the hat $25.
2. Fred is Jack's grandson.

Fun with Numbers
Malcolm had eight marbles, Robert twelve and Deborah sixteen.
The flour container weighs 4 ounces.
It is twenty-eight minutes past eight.

Odd Man Out
14; 16 (+2)
25; 30 (+5)
14; 17 (+2; +3)
31; 35 (+7; +4)
9; 3 (+3; −6)
19; 26 (−5; +7)
39.375; 4.921875 (x3; ÷4; x5; ÷6; etc.)
198.41; 24.8 (÷2; ÷3; ÷4; ÷5; etc.)
452 (doesn't divide by 3)

pages 14–15
Words and More Words
LOSE SOS EGGS BEES SHELLS

Pure Genius
1. 3,628,800
2. 20,000,000
3. Some ways of making 224:
222+2; 448÷2; 228−4; 896÷4.

Think of a Number
After a while no new numbers occur.

pages 16–17
Puzzle
With four lids it takes a minimum of fifteen moves.

pages 18-19
Tricky Triangles
The bottom right triangle contains the largest, the bottom left the smallest.

pages 20–21
Magic Squares

12	7	14
13	11	9
8	15	10

15	8	1	24	17
16	14	7	5	23
22	20	13	6	4
3	21	19	12	10
9	2	25	18	11

Three rows

8	1	6
4		2
3	5	7

pages 22–23
Numbers Galore

ODD × EVEN = EVEN
EVEN × EVEN = EVEN
ODD × ODD = ODD

pages 32–33
All identical?
Bottom plane.

Teacher's Problem
(air)

All the Same?
Ships 4 and 5.

pages 38–39
Names, Faces and Numbers
Can you put a name to these faces?

pages 40–41
Race Course Madness
True. Horatio Bottomley's race took place just before World War I at Blanckenburg, in Belgium.

Book Facts
1. True.
2. False: the heaviest book in the world weighs 555 pounds.
3. False: it is by Roald Dahl.
4. True.
5. True.

Fact or Fiction?
1. False: they are in South America.
2. True: its area is 64 million square miles.
3. True.
4. False: Mount Everest is in the Himalayas.
5. False: Helsinki is farther north than New York.
6. True: the dust from the explosion carried as far as London.
7. True: they are used to generate electricity.
8. False: Indonesia is too warm.
9. True.
10. False: it is nearly six miles high.

A Grave Face
No one really knows whether this story is true or not.

pages 42–43
Can It Be Done?
There were eighty-seven children at Shaun's party: twenty-nine took two pieces of candy, three took three pieces and fifty-five took one piece.

Roots
Geranium, Dandelion, Sunflower, Chrysanthemum, Pansy, Petunia, Tulip, Daisy, Rose, Marigold

pages 46–47
Codes and Ciphers
Meet me tonight.

pages 48–49
Using pictures
1. I can see you.
2. I have a pair of socks and some shoes.

Cryptic Clues
1. This is quite easy.
2. Mindbenders.

pages 50–51
Odd Man Out
Here are the odd ones.

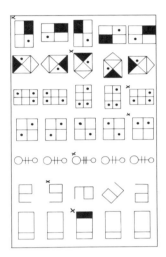

Three-Square

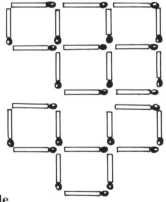

Puzzle
Move 4 to touch 5 and 6.
Move 5 the shortest distance to touch 1 and 2.
Move 1 to touch 4 and 5.

pages 58–59
Fruity Floaters
The peeled oranges will sink because the fruit inside is denser than the peel. The apple, banana and tomato will all float.

Problem Poser
The water beneath the boat provides upthrust, supporting the boat and preventing it from sinking.

pages 68–69
Reaction Time
The gap is caused by the time taken for the sound of the whistle to reach the runners, and for their brains to respond to that signal.

Problem
One million seconds

pages 70–71
Odd Ones
Sea gull (seabird)
yellow (all the others have five letters)
New York (all the others are capital cities)
bread (all the others are liquids)
son (all the others end in -er)

Missing Figures
1. 123 + 345 = 468
2. 265 + 324 = 589
3. 678 − 536 = 142
4. 25 x 5 = 125
5. 1000 + 1500 = 2500
6. 1500 − 1400 = 100
7. 20 x 7 = 140
8. 10 + 10 + 1180 = 1200
9. 6 x 30 = 180
10. 5 + 10 + 10 = 25

Family Tree
1. grandfather 2. sister 3. sister-in-law 4. niece 5. son 6. grandson

Vertices
The answer to the lettered shape is:
A-B, B-C, C-D, D-A, A-C, C-E, E-B, B-D.

Logic
1. John 2. Russian 3. Jessie 4. John

pages 80–81
How Many?
The lower drawing contains the most squares.

How Many Ways?
With four colors, 24 different ways.
With five colors, 120 different ways.

The Dice Game
The number one will never come up with two dice.

On and Off
There are 30 people on the bus.
There are 101 passengers left on the plane at Auckland.
There are no crows left. The rest flew away when they heard the shots.

Six, seven
1. 279,936 2. 117,649 3. 1764
4. 1111 5. 90,909
There will be 51 marbles.

pages 82–83
Match These
Leave lines spaces for diagrams.

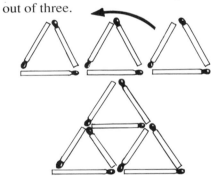

Here is Albert Crookfoot's pigpen. Here's how to make five triangles out of three.

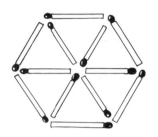

This makes NINE matches out of eleven.

pages 84–85
Sight Line
When you close one eye, you are seeing the finger farthest away from a different angle.

Disappearing Air
The candle needs the oxygen in the air in order to burn. Once it has used up all the oxygen in the jar, it goes out.

pages 86–87
Opposites
hot – cold
bad – good
open – closed
fat – thin
small – large
serious – funny
dangerous – safe
expand – contract
minute – huge
boring – interesting
baby – adult
nervous – confident
sober – drunk
tight – loose
violent – gentle

Family Problems
1. The boy is the man's nephew and the woman's son.
2. I am eighteen, my brother is twenty-three and my sister is sixteen.
3. I am nine.

Problems
1. I am thirteen.
2. Two dollars each. They were grandmother, mother and daughter.
3. Susie is twenty-six.
4. You don't bury survivors.

Coin Puzzles
A quarter and a dime. Only one of the coins is not a quarter!

Form the twelve coins into an equilateral triangle.

It takes eighteen moves to put the nickels where the dimes are in the shape, making one move at a time.

Time to Stop
1. 1:57 P.M.
2. 7:51
3. Five minutes late.
4. 11:36 P.M.
5. 3:02 P.M.

INDEX

Page numbers in *italics* refer to illustrated entries.